P9-AFA-191

AMERICAN HERITAGE
ILLUSTRATED HISTORY
OF THE UNITED STATES

Standing in the ghostly moonlight of the plains, the sentinel in Frederick Remington's painting watches for Indians and buffalo with his rifle cocked.
REMINGTON ART MUSEUM

FRONT COVER: *An Indian war party watches a wagon train, heading west, as it passes through its territory.*
LINDLEY AND CHARLES EBERSTADT COLLECTION OF WEBSTER PAINTINGS

FRONT ENDSHEET: *The Great Emigration of 1843 sent a wave of pioneers west. Albert Bierstadt painted this view of one caravan nearing its destination.*
BUTLER INSTITUTE OF AMERICAN ART

CONTENTS PAGE: *In a George Catlin painting, a war party, carrying hatchets and decorated shields, moves single file across the wide and barren plains.*

BACK ENDSHEET: *Cries and shouts fill the air as a war party rides around camp at the climax of its ceremonial preparation for battle with the enemy.*
COLLECTION OF HAROLD MCCRACKEN

BACK COVER: *Eager miners (top left) flocked to California when gold was discovered; Daniel Boone was the most famous of the pioneers of the old Southwest (top right); detail of painting of California settlers dancing the fandango (bottom).*
CROCKET ART MUSEUM; NATIONAL PORTRAIT GALLERY; LIBRARY OF CONGRESS

AMERICAN HERITAGE
ILLUSTRATED HISTORY
OF THE UNITED STATES

VOLUME 6

THE FRONTIER

BY ROBERT G. ATHEARN

Created in Association with the
Editors of AMERICAN HERITAGE
and for the updated edition
MEDIA PROJECTS INCORPORATED

CHOICE PUBLISHING, INC.
New York

© 1988, 1971, 1967, 1963 by American Heritage, a division of Forbes Inc. All rights reserved. No part of this work may be reproduced or transmitted in any form or by any means, electronic or mechanical, including photocopying and recording, or by any information storage or retrieval system without permission in writing from the publisher.

Library of Congress Catalog Card Number: 87-73399
ISBN 0-945260-06-7

This 1988 edition is published and distributed by Choice Publishing, Inc., 53 Watermill Lane, Great Neck, NY 11021
by arrangement with American Heritage, a division of Forbes, Inc.

Manufactured in the United States of America

CONTENTS OF THE COMPLETE SERIES

Editor's Note to the Revised Edition
Introduction by ALLAN NEVINS
Main text by ROBERT G. ATHEARN

EACH VOLUME CONTAINS AN ENCYCLOPEDIC SECTION; MASTER INDEX IN VOLUME 18

CONTENTS OF VOLUME 6

CHAPTER 16

MOVING WEST

By the Treaty of 1783 that ended the Revolution, the western boundary of the new nation was the Mississippi River. The settlers, no longer restricted by officials in London, immediately began to migrate in large numbers into the regions beyond the Appalachians. Their curiosity was the same as that of the early promoter who once asked of the Carolina frontier, "If the Porch be so beautiful, what must the Temple be?" Up to the War of 1812, the invasion of the Ohio River country and the land beyond was held partially in check by Indian opposition. The war broke the Indians' resistance, and after its conclusion, the defeated natives were forced back and the big land rush was on.

The westward movement is often considered in terms of a "frontier line" that progressed inexorably toward the Pacific Ocean. This artificial marker designated the boundary between the country having more than two people per square mile and that

Daniel Boone was the most famous of the pioneers of the Old Southwest. This print is from Chester Harding's 1819 portrait.

having fewer. In 1790, this line could have been found as far east as the Atlantic Ocean in parts of Maine. It skirted through Vermont, New Hampshire, eastern New York, eastern Pennsylvania, down through Virginia, and into the Carolinas. Of the 4,000,000 people living in the United States at that time, 94% were east of such a frontier line. By 1860, the same line ran through Wisconsin, Minnesota, Iowa, Nebraska, Kansas, and into Texas. By that time, too, another frontier line, across the Great Plains, had made an eastward indentation in California and Oregon on the Pacific Coast. The census taker of 1860 discovered there were then 31,500,000 people in the country, with about half of them living west of the Appalachians. California could claim more people in its decade as a state than New Hampshire had collected in all its history.

What were the reasons for such a growth? The chief inducement to the Western settler was cheap land. Those in the East, who saw available land disappear and prices rise, looked thoughtfully to the West, where land was not only more fertile but much

MISSOURI HISTORICAL SOCIETY

cheaper. Europeans also looked enviously toward Western America. In their part of the world, the soil had been worked for centuries. It was not common, furthermore, for the individual in the Old World to be able to own his own farm. Usually he was a tenant. The existence of limitless, inexpensive acres on the American frontiers was a powerful attraction to prospective immigrants. Further encouragement came from the belief that individual opportunity and freedom were greater under the democratic form of government. While this alone may not have been enough to induce a man to move, it perhaps helped him to make his decision as he thought about owning a farm of his own in the American West.

Before 1862, land was not free, but until then it had always been relatively low-priced. Under the Ordinance of 1785, the federal domain was to be divided into townships six miles square, each of them subdivided into 640-acre sections, one mile square. Sale was by auction, at $1 per acre, a difficult system for the small buyer. In 1796, a provision was made for credit, but the price was raised to $2 per acre. Although Easterners thought this reasonable, it was too expensive for many frontiersmen. Loud complaints brought another change in 1800. Now the farmer could buy as few as 320 acres, and land offices were set up closer to the Western tracts. But the price was not lowered. Agitation continued until the minimum size

of farms was again reduced and the price was cut. The new law of 1820 allowed a man to buy as few as 80 acres at $1.25 per acre. This meant that $100 would buy a farm. It also indicated that the government policy had shifted from one of trying to make money from the public domain to one that emphasized locating farmers on the land. Yet a cash payment of $100 was still a burden to the pioneer, and most Western lands continued to be bought for speculation rather than settlement.

In 1841, another concession was given to the land-hungry. The Preemption Act provided that a man could settle upon land not yet opened for sale and still have the first chance at his own tract when surveys were made. In other words, "squatting" was legalized. Then, in 1862, the Homestead Act offered a quarter section of 160 acres free to a person who would settle and make certain improvements. Any adult citizen, or adult person declaring his intention to become a citizen, was eligible. It is small wonder that thousands of people in Europe and America began to think of pulling up stakes and heading west.

Establishing a new home in the West was not as easy as it appeared, however. The encouragements were great, but practical difficulties stood in the way. The main barrier, particularly during the early years of American experience, was a lack of adequate transportation. Roads were few, and those in existence were usu-

Two early settlers, on the trail with their covered wagons, try to yoke an ox that struggles to elude them, in a scene painted by William Henry Jackson.

ally wretched. Until the decade of the 1850s, there were also few railroads west of the Appalachians, and they were of little value to the settler. The best avenues of transportation, before the day of the canals and railroads, were the Ohio and Mississippi Rivers and their many tributaries. The Great Lakes, of course, had long been used in the westward movement.

It is true that a pioneer family, given enough time, could work its way across an unfriendly land to settle in some remote spot. But that did not solve a problem; it created one. Far from markets, the settler had no easy way to sell his agricultural products, unless he could use the rivers. But not every farm was near a navigable stream. This meant that the farmer was often forced to use up his own produce, and in such circumstances he was not likely to raise much more than his family required. Such "subsistence" living was severely limiting.

The situation presented by the Indian was also significant. From the outset, the natives were disturbed by the growing number of whites and by their hunger for land. The inevitable clash lasted from the time of the Pequot War in New England in 1637 to the final battles on the Great Plains and in the Southwest near the close of the 19th century. The whites had on their side the advantage of numbers and the superior weapons of an industrialized nation, but at

457

One of the many shiploads of 19th-century Irish immigrants fleeing the potato famine debarks at New York City. In the harbor is the Keying, *which claimed to be the first Chinese ship to visit America.*

times they had a two-front problem. Ahead were resisting Indians, and behind on occasion were governments that tried to restrain their encroachments on the natives' lands. How the whites overran the continent is not a pretty story. It is one of deceit, of cruelty on both sides, of lawbreaking, and of the final triumph of a stronger people. Today sympathies are largely with the Indians, but that is not much consolation to the dispossessed.

Another obstacle to westward expansion was financial. Then, as now, it took money to move a family. Before 1862, land cost $1.25 an acre, and, even supposing a satisfactory farm could be had for that figure, additional funds were needed to pay expenses until the first crop could be harvested. Moreover, the frontier was a place of speculation and inflation. The result was often a roller-coaster economy that climbed to great heights and then plunged in violent descents. When financial panics came—as they did in 1819 and 1837—the severest kind of depressions staggered the Western economy. Many pioneer families were driven back to the East, bankrupt and thoroughly disheartened. Where instability was worst, whole communities were virtually wiped out, and the frontier line was halted until the settlers' forces could gather strength for a fresh assault.

Despite all discouragements, the westward movement persisted. Its main body was resolute farmers who accustomed themselves to privation and suffering, whether from isolation, Indians, or monetary fluctuation. They came from New England, whose changing economy and thin topsoil drove them to search for new and better land. Southerners, faced by increasing competition from large, slaveholding landowners, moved west in search of a more favorable competitive situation. Europeans, tired of political turmoil and economic disruptions, joined the westward-moving

MUSEUM OF THE CITY OF NEW YORK

agrarian army. So great was the influx that one prominent New York merchant was moved to complain, "All Europe is coming across the ocean—all that part at least who cannot make a living at home—and what shall we do with them?" He need not have been worried, for at that time—during the 1830s—few of the newcomers tarried long in the Eastern port cities. The magnetic attraction of land drew them on, through the mountain passes, down the slopes of the Appalachians, and out toward the great Mississippi Valley.

The new West welcomed these strangers. Young states, eager for growth and political importance, employed immigration commissioners whose business it was to publicize their part of the country. Thousands of pamphlets poured out of their offices, printed in different European languages. The smallest villages in Germany, Ireland, Switzerland, and Scandinavia became acquainted with economic possibilities in remote places like Wisconsin, Illinois, and Indiana. By 1860, the census revealed that the percentage of aliens in the state of Wisconsin was larger than that of Eastern districts and that a goodly number of Eastern-born people had moved to Western homes—a fact that

459

disturbed Atlantic-seaboard communities whose population was being drained away. Vermonters, for example, noticed that while their population stood almost still, such upstart areas as Iowa grew by more than 250% during the 1850s.

Western life

Isolation from the Atlantic seaboard tended to make Westerners look to the South. Those along the Ohio and Mississippi Rivers regarded New Orleans as their chief market, for it was no great task to build crude plank flatboats upon which farmers could float downriver with tons of produce. There they sold their crops, knocked apart the flatboats, sold the planks, and returned home. This commercial necessity early gave the West, from Minnesota to Louisiana, a unity that only the Civil War would disrupt.

Distance from market, and distance from one's neighbors, had the effect of continuing and even magnifying the earlier-developed characteristics of independence and self-reliance. The farther west the frontier moved, and the more remote its settlements, the greater was its tendency to mold men who were not only self-sustaining but

LILLY LIBRARY, INDIANA UNIVERSITY

often strong-willed about conducting their affairs as they saw fit. Thus isolation, although it presented problems, also shaped a society whose ideas and practices affected later generations of Westerners as well as the nation itself.

Until the frontier farmer reached the prairies of Minnesota and Iowa, he was obliged to spend most of his time clearing trees from the land in order to plant his crops. Agricultural life must often have seemed a nightmare of blackened stumps that defied the plow. So tree-conscious did the farmer become that when he emerged from the wooded regions and came upon open patches of land, he could not believe that the soil was as good as that of the forested lands. Yet when he left behind the timbered country and moved onto the rolling, treeless prairies of the West, he discovered that the tree had not been without its virtues. Now he remembered that it had supplied him with many of his necessities. Split-rail fences, log houses, pole-lined walls—indeed, the old oaken bucket itself—had come from his groves. So had his benches, tables, beds, floors, and even his clay-lined log fireplace. Fuel for fires had never been a problem to him before. Now he faced a country without wood.

Wherever the frontiersman lived, he was also burdened with the problem of defense. Normally he provided his own. Government—national, state, or county—was traditionally unable to give adequate protection against the resentful Indians. Nor could government always control lawless whites, especially where the countryside was thinly populated. Many pioneer agrarians worked at their daily tasks encumbered by their heavy rifles.

In the beginning, Western justice was necessarily swift and violent. Men solved legal problems directly and in an individual way. Their code was somewhat different from ours, but it developed out of the exigencies

Drifting down with the river's current is a loaded flatboat, and pushing its way up the river is what replaced it as a carrier of cargo, the great steamboat.

461

The frontier created powerful and fantastic folk heroes who fitted its incredible characteristics, like this boatman driving two harnessed water monsters.

of the time. To understand why sudden death was the penalty for horse-stealing, one must remember that loss of a horse might mean mortal danger to its owner. Men were punished by floggings and banishment because communities often did not have jails and penitentiaries.

Because the frontier was essentially agricultural, day-to-day existence was generally drab and uninteresting. It was a life of dawn-to-dusk work ridding the fields of timber and rocks, sowing, cultivating, and harvesting crops, and getting a bare livelihood in return. Little time or energy remained for pursuits of the mind. Men's values tended to be more practical and mate-

BROOKLYN MUSEUM

Timber cleared from the land was used in many ways, as material for the split-rail fence and as lumber for the log cabin.

rial. In religion, frontier families wanted exhilaration rather than contemplation. Understandably, the revival movement captured their attention and interest, for they could appreciate both its direct approach and its action.

Despite their long hours of labor, the frontier people did not altogether ignore the cultural side of life. But they did not have much opportunity to make original contributions to native literature, drama, or music. Except for occasional folk music, about all they could do was mimic the East and try to reproduce its civilization as they knew it. They were conscious of their deficiencies, yet the slightest inference of any cultural lag aroused instant animosity.

Perhaps the Westerners' realization of their cultural isolation explains

463

Women's seminaries were in existence by the early 1800s. Here, at graduation exercises, a wreath is placed on the head of one of the honor students.

their efforts to compensate. Great value was attached to books, and no small amount of respect was given to those with "book learning," although this feeling was kept well hidden. A surprising number of log homes had copies of *Pilgrim's Progress* and other classic works. The family Bible was treasured as literature as well as a family archive where births and deaths were recorded. Newspapers and almanacs also were found in many homes. Villages tried—and often failed—to support local newspapers, for they were the chief mediums of intellectual communication on the frontier.

Most Westerners privately admitted that an education was a worthy and desirable achievement, but to gain it was both difficult and expensive. The common man had to content himself with the most rudimentary kind of learning. A minimum acquaintance with the basic "three Rs" sufficed to carry on what simple business transactions confronted him, and there was little necessity to rise above this level. When children had learned to read, write, and do simple arithmetic, there was a tendency to take them from the classroom and put them to some of the many tasks required by a growing economy. More extended education was often opposed on the ground that it was too costly in time and money. Private schools struggled against this

464

COLLECTION OF EDGAR WILLIAM AND BERNICE CHRYSLER GARBISCH

attitude, and even public schools, praised as a matter of policy, were damned because they increased taxes. Sometimes higher education received attention only because church organizations were willing to appropriate money for the construction and maintenance of buildings. But even these efforts did not serve many students. Before 1800, Transylvania University at Lexington, Kentucky, was the only institution of higher learning west of the Appalachians, and its struggle for existence was nothing short of heroic. To the Westerner, learning was a laudable achievement, but he viewed it as a social frill to be added only after the fulfillment of the family's material needs.

As people of an area characterized by hard physical labor, frontiersmen quickly became scornful of those who did not work with their hands. Even the preacher and the teacher took their turns at manual labor and thereby found a place in the hearts of their neighbors. There were, of course, practical reasons for this participation, for there was not enough labor in most Western communities to support nonproducers. In the hardworking, isolated society there also developed a general disdain for Europeans, who seemed to be regarded by Westerners as aristocrats and snobs. This rejection of the old country helped mold the newcomers into a breed that became even more antiEuropean than the residents of the Atlantic seaboard. So strong was the feeling that it became a part of the American heritage.

When the United States won its freedom from Great Britain, it faced a number of difficult problems. One was administering Western lands that had not yet been organized into states. Americans, who had just ended their successful fight against the British colonial system, did not regard their Western possessions as colonies. But when the new nation chose to govern those lands from Washington, even through appointed "territorial" governors, judges, and other officials, many frontiersmen saw a parallel to the British imperial policy and protested vehemently.

Uncle Sam's stepchildren

There was one outstanding difference between the two systems. The Northwest Ordinance of 1787, enacted even before the writing of the Constitution, set at rest some of the fears that the federal Congress would forever withhold self-government from parts of the nation. It said a territory could enter the Union upon fulfilling certain requirements. When its free adult male population reached 5,000, it could elect a legislature. It could send to Congress a delegate who could make speeches, but could not vote. When its population reached 60,000 free inhabitants, application for statehood could be made.

Despite the promise of eventual statehood, guaranteed again when the Constitution was adopted, many fron-

MINNEAPOLIS INSTITUTE OF ARTS

Fort Snelling, Minnesota, painted by the soldier-artist Seth Eastman in the 1840s, was for more than 30 years the army's farthest Northwest outpost.

SOCIETY OF CALIFORNIA PIONEERS

tiersmen felt that their pre-Revolution problems were not wholly solved. Each new westward wave of people put the outer edge of civilization farther from the central government at Washington. As the distance grew, so did a feeling of resentment toward those who governed from afar. Complaints against appointed officials were frequent. The federal army, charged with the task of protecting remote settlements against the Indians, was subject to bitter criticism for its short-

comings. It was easy for those engaged in pioneering to believe they were political stepchildren, neglected and forgotten by a self-indulgent parent.

The most important result of this attitude was the inclination of territorial residents to shift for themselves, just as the colonials had during England's period of "salutary neglect." When the army failed to live up to expectations in punishing marauding Indians, Westerners went into action.

Volunteers, led by governors who were often ambitious politicians in search of fame, took to the field to eliminate the Indian enemy. Sometimes this led to warfare of such proportions that federal help was needed to restore peace, but the territorial people looked upon this simply as evidence of the government's original laxity.

Westerners were also likely to take political matters into their own hands. During the 1770s, some of them set up a local government along Tennessee's Watauga River and went into business for themselves. Formulating Articles of Association, they elected 13 representatives, who in turn appointed five commissioners to operate the new government. It was as spontaneous as the Mayflower Compact 150 years earlier. It was a body politic, born full-grown, ready and able to govern itself. Three-quarters of a century later, in 1859, Colorado miners would organize miniature governments in

Vigilante headquarters in San Francisco in 1856 was called Fort Gunnybags because of its fortifications. Note the accusing eye on the official seal.

mining camps yet untouched by the long arm of Eastern law. The propensity to write constitutions and set up governments ran strong among the frontiersmen. They were a great do-it-yourself people.

Significance of the frontier

Before the Mexican War, the country called the West extended from the Appalachian Mountains to a line not far across the Mississippi River. This was the area of settlement and of agricultural development. The land beyond was vaguely called the Far West. It was the haunt of the Indian, the trapper, and the occasional explorer. Economically, it was not yet significant. By the Louisiana Purchase of 1803, the United States acquired the remote reaches between the Mississippi and the Rockies, but little could be done at once to develop that territory. The nation was not ready.

Although settlement of the Western plains was delayed, the region we call the Midwest was rapidly populated between 1815 and the 1840s. Migration into this region had important influences upon the nation at large. It provided a growing market for Eastern manufactures and encouraged the rising industrial areas to develop all possible means of transportation to and from the West. Both influences were accelerated when settlers moved onto the treeless plains, where they required outside help to get fencing, lumber, furniture, and hardware. Once the farmer moved to where he could market his crops for cash, his dependence upon manufactures grew fast. He became highly important to Eastern businessmen, who regarded him as a prime prospect.

Socially, the great advance of settlement had the effect of increasing the Americanization process typical of the frontier. As the leveling influence touched larger numbers, the nation felt its effect, for by now the West was much more powerful in Congress. Western members thundered their ideologies throughout legislative halls, and the "little people" the length and breadth of the land listened. Thus the social influences of the frontier had their effect upon political growth. The common man, wherever he was, came to demand a greater share in government, and during the Jackson era in particular the movement reached epic proportions.

Finally, the growth of the Mississippi and Ohio River Valleys set the scene for the next big move westward. It provided a training ground for those who would go on. Although some adjustments had to be made for the assault upon a new kind of land, where agricultural practices would have to be modified, it was a good place to learn the trade. The nation at large looked on and approved of such successful expansion. When the day came for Americans to make the great leap across the plains to Oregon and California, they would be ready, for by then "westering" had become a part of the national tradition.

KNOEDLER GALLERIES

THE GREAT GOLD RUSH

January 24, 1848, when James Marshall found gold in the race of the sawmill he was building for John Sutter, is an important date in the history of California and the West. This chance discovery was to set off the biggest and the gaudiest gold rush ever—and, ironically, was to leave both Marshall and Sutter broke at the end of their lives. Sutter, fearing that his land would be overrun when word of the discovery was circulated, did his best to hush up the news and keep miners away. At first many *were* skeptical, not realizing the extent of the bonanza. Then, in May, a huckstering genius named Sam Brannan —a Mormon businessman who saw a chance to make a fortune by building a store for the miners near Sutter's mill—appeared in San Francisco, waving a bottle full of gold dust and shouting, "Gold! Gold from the American River!" His electrifying performance produced a frenzy. In about a week, crowds of people began to go to Sutter's mill. San Francisco became, for a time, a ghost town, and as word spread, thousands flocked to the gold fields from every part of the world. The great gold rush was on, and the lust to get rich quick consumed the minds of men from all walks of life. Typical of the many who sought gold is the quartet above, using both a pan and a cradle.

EDWARD EBERSTADT & SONS

JOHN AUGUSTUS SUTTER

GOLD!
GOLD!
GOLD!

It was at John Sutter's sawmill (below), on the bank of the American River at Coloma, that his building foreman, James Marshall, first discovered gold.

COLLECTION OF ROBERT HONEYMAN

CARL S. DENTZEL

When the gold rush began, the trading post at Sutter's Fort (above) was the center of John Sutter's private empire. As gold seekers swarmed over his land, and his help ran away to the diggings, his holdings vanished. But Sam Brannan, who had proclaimed the discovery, became a rich man.

JAMES MARSHALL
CALIFORNIA STATE LIBRARY

SAM BRANNAN
CALIFORNIA HISTORICAL SOCIETY

The famous nugget that Marshall took from Sutter's mill is actually only dime-size.

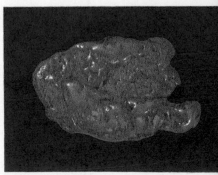

UNIVERSITY OF CALIFORNIA

471

THE GREAT GOLD RUSH

CALIFORNIA, HERE THEY COME!

STATE STREET BANK AND TRUST COMPANY, BOSTON

The frantic pursuit of gold is mocked by N. Currier in this 1849 print with the title, *The Way They Go to California*. The prospectors (right) scream for places on steamers and more fantastic conveyances like the rocket and balloon.

HOW THEY MINED GOLD

LOS ANGELES COUNTY MUSEUM

This prospector is using a washbowl, or pan, to take gold out of the sand of a creek bed. The principle of gold panning depends on the fact that gold is about eight times as heavy as sand and will sink to the bottom of the pan while the lighter sand is spilled over the edge by the water. The process was inefficient and many flakes of gold were lost.

ZELDA MACKAY COLLECTION, BANCROFT LIBRARY

Because group ventures had more chance of success, the day of the individual miner soon passed. In the daguerreotype above, six men operate a gravel-washing machine called a cradle. Such devices could handle far greater amounts of gold-bearing dirt than a miner with a pan.

The Long Tom (right) was a trough with a piece of perforated sheet iron at one end. Water from a stream ran through constantly, washing the dirt that was shoveled in. Cleats in a "ripple box" underneath the iron sheet then caught the heavy flakes of gold as they settled.

OVERLEAF: The larger the gravel-washing machines became, the more water their operation required. Groups of miners often cooperated to build systems of water wheels like this one at Cut Eye Foster's Bar on the North Yuba River in California that supplied water for Long Toms.

COLLECTION OF ROBERT HONEYMAN

CALIFORNIA STATE LIBRARY

475

HARSH JUSTICE

ALL: COLLECTION OF ROBERT HONEYMAN

As there was often no one to protect them from robbery and violence, gold seekers were moved to take the law into their own hands. In the painting above, an accused horse thief (standing, center, in long coat) is tried in a miner's cabin.

The forty-niner who would rather steal his gold than dig for it is caricatured at the left. Such men were dealt with harshly. In the miners' courts, the penalties ranged from hanging for the large thefts and murder to flogging for petty crimes.

Joaquin Murrieta (right) terrorized California during the gold rush with a series of murders, stagecoach holdups, and cattle thefts. After he was killed in 1853, his head was exhibited in a bottle.

CALIFORNIA HISTORICAL SOCIETY

THE GREAT GOLD RUSH

IT WAS NOT ALL WORK

E. B. CROCKER ART GALLERY

GENE AUTRY

Hangtown (above, left)—or Placerville, as it is now known—acquired its unsavory name when three robbers were strung up from a tree in its main street. One of many gold-rush boom towns, it was once California's third-largest settlement.

The absence of women in remote mining camps did not prevent forty-niners from holding an occasional fandango, like the abandoned affair above. "Ladies" were designated by a patch on their pants or a handkerchief worn on their sleeves.

Sunday was for some a time of rest and contemplation; for others an excuse to continue Saturday night's binge. In the painting at the left, a brawl erupts, a horse race is run, and a miner celebrates a strike. The men in the center write home or listen to a Bible reading. At the right, a miner washes what remains of his pants.

481

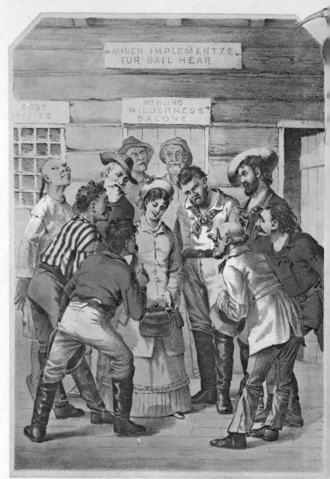

COLLECTION OF ROBERT HONEYMAN

THE GREAT GOLD RUSH

MEN
WITHOUT
WOMEN

NEW-YORK HISTORICAL SOCIETY

LIBRARY OF CONGRESS

"Married, Mum?" is the question women-starved prospectors are asking a pretty young lady who has just arrived in their mining camp, in the German lithograph at the left, above. At the right she gives her encouraging and well-received reply: "No, sir!" The dancing girl (above, far right) traveled with one of the many vaudeville shows that had become a regular fixture in the gold fields by the late 1850s.

Men of many nations sought their fortunes in California. At the left, Mexican rancheros, American miners, and Chinese laborers mingle in a San Francisco bar.

Away from the pleasures (and restraints) of wife and family, gold seekers often sought solace in the saloon. At the right, three prospectors enjoy a friendly nip.

NEW-YORK HISTORICAL SOCIETY

483

A BOOM TOWN'S PROGRESS

NEW-YORK HISTORICAL SOCIETY

As prospectors poured into California, new towns appeared by the score. None grew with greater abandon than bawdy San Francisco, the port city that was the gateway to the mining country. When the influx began, the one-time Spanish settlement was so unprepared for it that hundreds had to camp in tents on Telegraph Hill (above). While buildings went up, the streets (left) remained a morass of mud. But by the 1860s, when the daguerreotype at the right was taken, the city had little resemblance to the village of 800 people that it had been just before the gold rush.

484

WELLS FARGO BANK AND UNION TRUST COMPANY

AMERICAN ANTIQUARIAN SOCIETY

CHAPTER 17

CRUSADES AND CULTURE

The nation's physical expansion during the years that followed the War of 1812 had a deeper meaning than merely an increase of population and industrial development. As the American people witnessed a growing economic independence from Great Britain and Europe, and counted the new Western states entering the Union, they experienced a swelling pride in what the world called the great democratic experiment. To the national structure, they now wished to add some of the refinements of society without which the job could not be regarded as properly finished.

The large cities grew along the East Coast, and for a long time theaters, libraries, schools, and other evidences of cultural interest and support were centered there. Westerners, absorbed in carving out an empire, and necessarily concerned with the day-to-day problems of living, were at first inclined to jeer at Eastern cultural efforts. This was merely an admission of their own shortcomings. As soon as

New York's Park Theatre in 1829 had no rule against wearing hats or standing in the orchestra. But ladies sat upstairs.

possible, they tried to acquire some of the refinements of life for themselves, usually copying their Eastern brothers. Most of the plays and concerts in the West were imported from the East or from Europe. Only when Western communities had passed the frontier stage did any native talent emerge.

Accompanying the intellectual ferment and increased democratization of the first half of the 19th century was a strong humanitarian surge. Suddenly America found itself fascinated by reform in every part of life. The movement had some of its roots in a revulsion against the evils revealed in industrial England, where labor, depressed and discontented, began to react violently. As yet, America had not developed a proletariat—a propertyless working class—of any size. Nevertheless, its factory system already had begun to breed social inequalities to which believers in Jacksonian democracy objected. In an era when the rights of man were so greatly stressed, anyone with a grievance against the more entrenched members of the established order found listeners.

The emphasis of reform, however, was not upon the plight of the work-

NEW-YORK HISTORICAL SOCIETY

ing class. That would have been an admission of guilt by factory owners, and even in this early day the public believed that industrial development must in no way be disturbed. Businessmen were willing to lend a sympathetic ear to the woes of the underprivileged, as long as their troubles were not associated with the conditions of their employment. Reformers were directed to other fertile fields, such as the improvement of conditions among the blind, deaf, insane, poor, and imprisoned.

Humanitarian impulses

Pauperism was one of the economic ills that required attention. In a land of plenty it had no justifiable place. Also, the pauper's prison was an inheritance from England that now came to be regarded as unwelcome and un-American. Many states abolished imprisonment for debt. City fathers of rising industrial towns were moved to provide breadlines and other charitable aids in the face of growing unevenness of employment. They saw the alternative as one of violence if the workers were pushed too far, and they responded as much

This actionful lithograph shows Jenny Lind, "The Swedish Nightingale," sleighing past P.T. Barnum's American Museum in New York City. It was Barnum, the great promoter of the unusual, who brought the famous soprano to America for the first time in 1850, and she was a tremendous success. She had clothing, furniture, and even a clipper ship named after her.

RINGLING MUSEUM OF THE CIRCUS

488

out of fear as out of philanthropy. That they acted at all is perhaps to their credit.

The lot of other unfortunates was considerably alleviated during these years. As the nation became larger and its law-enforcement agencies improved, prisons grew crowded. There was a recognized need for the improvement of conditions in public institutions, as well as for the reclassification of persons who were arrested. For years paupers, the insane, petty offenders, and professional criminals had been thrown together indiscriminately. New institutions were established for the mentally ill, the blind, the deaf, and for others who were handicapped. There was also an increasing tendency to regard them as wards of the state, rather than to rely upon the uncertain efforts of private charities or allow those needing care or treatment to stay with their families, who were often unable to meet their needs.

One of the oldest and most persistent American crusades for reform was the temperance movement. There were hundreds of local societies as early as the 1830s, and during that decade a national organization called the United States Temperance Union appeared. Some of the groups had odd origins. One was the Washingtonians, whose fighting core sprang from a small number of alcoholics in Baltimore. One night in 1840, the revelers staggered into a temperance meeting in that city and were so im-

NEW YORK PUBLIC LIBRARY

"Father, come home," pleads a child in Ten Nights in a Barroom, *a novel that won converts for temperance in the 1850s.*

pressed by the earnestness of the reformers that they retreated to a tavern and founded a new temperance society. Taking the name of the country's first President, they dedicated themselves to alcoholic moderation. The initiation fee was set at 25¢, and monthly dues at half that figure. A few years later, the society published the *Washingtonian Teetotaler's Minstrel,* a songbook that contained such deathless classics as *Dear Father, Drink No More* and *Mother, Dry That*

Flowing Tear. Most famous of the temperance books, however, was Timothy Shay Arthur's *Ten Nights in a Barroom,* published in 1854. It was adapted for dramatic presentation and came near rivaling *Uncle Tom's Cabin* for sustained popularity.

Another part of the reform movement—one regarded with little enthusiasm by the male population—was the demand by women for equality. Since the days of Benjamin Franklin and Thomas Paine, a few intellectuals had taken the position that the shackles of tradition, rather than a natural mental inferiority, kept women in a secondary position. Such notions were regarded by the masculine majority as much too advanced, if not downright dangerous. They insisted that woman's place was in the home, away from public view, and that her first jobs were domestic duties and childbearing.

During the second quarter of the 19th century, the voice of womanhood was loud in the general outcry against special privilege. Although the women heard from were a small minority, their complaints echoed across the land. One militant feminist, Amelia Bloomer, who edited a temperance reform journal called *The Lily,* sought to dramatize her demand for equality by wearing mannish attire. She appeared in public in a short overskirt, reaching only to the unmentionable region of the knee, with pantaloons tied discreetly at the ankles to cover her lower extremities. Naturally, it caused a sensation. Elizabeth Cady Stanton, another of the feminine progressives, adopted a similar outfit and wore it in the face of considerable derision from street urchins who followed her about, chanting uncomplimentary doggerel.

By verbal bombardment and public nagging the women made some progress. John Greenleaf Whittier and Ralph Waldo Emerson of the literary world, and Wendell Phillips and William Lloyd Garrison, prominent abolitionists, came to their support. Even Abraham Lincoln, a young politician out in Illinois, declared he had no objection to sharing government with women. Before long some of the states began to relax their laws, permitting women to hold property and to be freed of liability for their husbands' debts. As a dividend, the movement produced a greater interest in the rights of children, whose increasing exploitation in factories was becoming a matter of national concern.

The antislavery crusade

Climaxing the humanitarian movements of the period was the crusade against human slavery. By the early 19th century, there was an increasing feeling through most of the country that something ought to be done to check the spread of what was generally regarded as an evil.

When the American Colonization Society was founded in 1816 to relocate free blacks abroad, it found support among humanitarians in both North and South. John Randolph of Virginia and William H. Crawford, another prominent Southerner, were active in it. At one time Henry Clay of Kentucky was its president. Although the society did not succeed in sending any appreciable number of slaves out of the country, or cope with the fundamental problem of black freedom, its existence tended for a time to satisfy the more moderate antislave groups. By the 1830s, interest in the abolition of slavery had sharply declined across the cotton belt, but in the North, particularly in New England, the movement was beginning to rise to the peak it would reach in the Civil War.

There were two reasons for a shift in Southern attitudes toward slavery. First, as new Southwestern lands were opened to growing cotton, the institution became more profitable to plantation owners. With the world price of cotton maintaining high levels and with an increasing availability of cotton-growing land, the Southerner found more use for slave labor than he had at an earlier time. The second reason for a stiffening defense of slavery was the extreme abolitionist stand taken by a small group of Northern crusaders. Their attitude that all slaveholders were moral lepers deeply angered Southerners, whether or not they owned slaves. This response, partly psychological, stemmed from the South's agrarian tradition, which was pastoral and antimercantile. Many Southerners feared that if they abandoned slavery, they themselves would become slaves of Northeastern industrial capitalism.

As in all great crusades, leadership was provided by tough-minded, outspoken individuals wholly dedicated to the cause. William Lloyd Garrison was typical. The young man first came to notice as an employee of Benjamin Lundy, publisher of a Baltimore abolitionist journal. Put in jail for printing libelous statements, Garrison stayed there seven weeks before being bailed out by a wealthy philanthropist. Thoroughly aroused, the newly freed printer hastened to Boston, where he started his own paper, *The Liberator*. In its first issue, January 1, 1831, Garrison took his stand, from which he never wavered. Contending that he did not wish to think, speak, or write with moderation upon the subject of abolition, he declared angrily, "I am in earnest—I will not equivocate—I will not excuse—I will not retreat a single inch—and *I will be heard*." He called the Constitution "a covenant with death and an agreement with hell," and swore that he would rather see the Union destroyed than to see it countenance the institution of slavery.

Garrison's literary blasts got attention from both supporters and enemies, but it was Theodore Weld, working in the Midwest, who made the most converts. His followers got many of their beliefs from the religious revivals of Charles G. Finney during the 1820s, and now, led by Weld, the group emphasized the religious-moral aspect of slavery, holding the institution to be a moral sin. Weld had more skill than Garrison in both organizing and publicizing. Whereas Garrison often antagonized prospective converts, Weld was more persuasive, even extending his efforts to Congress, where he helped to form an antislavery bloc. Many of the young reformer's followers were students at Oberlin College, founded in Ohio in 1833. It was one of the first American institutions of higher learning to admit black students and was also the first to admit women, in 1835. Modern studies have shown that Weld probably accomplished as much for his cause as the dogmatic Garrison did.

It was not unnatural that such a controversial issue should make its way into politics. In 1840, its adherents formed the Liberty Party and nominated James G. Birney, an abolitionist writer, for President. But in the national election, Birney got only slightly more than 7,000 votes, mostly in New England. Considering the general hostility to abolitionist extremism, it is perhaps surprising that he did that well. In time, however, increasing numbers of Northerners convinced themselves that the aristocratic masters of the South should be curbed, and the trend to vote against these political Bourbons grew. The important point of the antislavery crusade is that the feelings it aroused mounted steadily until it had gained a significant number of followers. By the time Lincoln ran for the Presi-

Amelia Bloomer and her followers, who wanted equal rights for women, advocated a more mannish style of costume. It caused ridicule, but its full trousers gave the word "bloomers" to the language.

ADDISON GALLERY OF AMERICAN ART

Public schools were generally accepted by the mid-19th century, and the teacher of that time was allowed to use the rod liberally in educating the student.

dency, the crusade against "social evils" was a potent political weapon.

The little red schoolhouse

Along with improved conditions among men and women of all classes came more interest in education. Particular emphasis was put on free education—a principle not as readily approved as modern students might suppose. But by the mid-19th century, state-supported schools were generally accepted, especially in the North and West. Children of the wealthy were still likely to be found in private schools, but it was no longer a mark of financial inability if one's children attended public institutions.

The explanation for the wide acceptance of public education is found in the determined crusade of those who believed in its virtues. Representative of those who felt strongly was a youthful Michigan judge who, as early as 1806, urged the creation of a public school system in that new territory. He argued that it would "advance the future prosperity of the country and the happiness of millions yet unborn." Hundreds of other farseeing Americans whose names are forgotten gave support to this part of the nation's further democratization. As in all movements, some individuals stood out. Horace Mann devoted a lifetime to the improvement of educational facilities and the expansion of the school curriculum. The inclusion of such subjects as music and hygiene was met with stubborn opposition by those who thought the young were unnecessarily pampered.

Henry Barnard was another leader in the field. He was instrumental in establishing the first state teachers' association, in 1845, and in the founding of the *American Journal of Education.* Later he helped to start the University of Wisconsin.

Literary growth

Before 1815, a good part of the literature read in this country was produced in England. Haughtily a British journal of 1820 asked the unkind question, "In the four quarters of the globe, who reads an American book?" Often the books published on this side of the Atlantic were pirated editions of English works. Charles Dickens was only one of the Victorian writers who strongly protested our refusal to recognize British copyright laws and the consequent loss of royalties to authors.

As part of their general declaration of independence, Americans eventually began to write and publish their own books. James Fenimore Cooper was said to have written his first novel, in 1820, as the result of a boast that he could turn out a better book than the English product he was reading. He determined to write a strictly American story. In *The Spy* he was eminently successful. His depiction of the American Indian in the *Leatherstocking Tales* deeply impressed Europeans, who regarded our natives as examples of Rousseau's man of nature, the *beau savage.* The sentimentally idealized Cooper Indian became so fixed in the minds of readers that the image is still with us today. The Lone Ranger's Tonto and Red Ryder's Little Beaver are modern examples of the type.

A few years after Cooper began writing, Ralph Waldo Emerson underscored the trend toward a native literature when he commented, "Let us have done with Europe and dead cultures, let us explore the possibilities of our own new world." Emerson, Henry David Thoreau, and a number of others including Orestes Brownson, Margaret Fuller, Theodore Parker, Bronson Alcott, and George Bancroft created a school of literature and thought known as Transcendentalism. They believed that moral law transcended natural law, that the knowledge of truth—implanted by God— transcended experience and reason. Their beliefs helped them to justify in their own minds the ideal of individual freedom—something rather easy for the inheritors of New England Puritanism with its faith in man's capacity for personal spiritual insight. Out of this school came a torrent of writing critical of an America that, to the Transcendentalists, was not living up to its potentialities. A tangible example of their belief was the establishment of Brook Farm in Massachusetts, one of a number of experiments in community living.

The social and intellectual stirrings, so apparent during the years that followed our second war with Great Britain, were indications of an emerging American nationality. Not only were we issuing declarations of independence—some of them perhaps unconsciously—in all aspects of daily life, but we were also turning our backs on Europe, determined to show the world that a new people had joined the community of nations. It was an era of vigorous, even boisterous, "Americanism."

The American character

Out of the great democratic surge came a widespread desire for social, economic, and political equality. Seemingly, every man aspired to be a member of the middle class. Certainly no one would admit that he belonged to the masses, and few would openly claim aristocratic origins. To dramatize the quest for the ordinary, it became fashionable to denounce the inequalities of other systems of government. Monarchy, for example, was regarded as a decadent relic of antiquity, based upon custom and privilege, and thoroughly out of date. Although Americans would sometimes boast privately that their family origins could be traced to high places in the old country, they saw nothing inconsistent in sneering at the institution of royalty. It was the democratic thing to do.

The cult of equalitarianism was a source of constant surprise to foreign visitors in America. Outwardly the citizens of the great democracy tended to look much alike in their dress. The similarity arose perhaps more because of the fact that in this country there were as yet no real extremes of poverty or wealth, rather than from any studied desire for sartorial democracy. However, the situation must have helped the people of lower income brackets feel that they had no decided superiors.

Along with this insistence upon personal equality there appeared a sentiment that seemed to run counter to it. The desire to achieve some kind of rank, to set oneself off from one's fellows, was everywhere. Coats of arms, reminiscent of European royalty, not only flourished but were so garishly elaborate that the self-respecting aristocrat on the other side of the Atlantic would have been embarrassed to have anything similar. Honorary titles were eagerly sought. Villages were overrun with men called Cap, Colonel, or Judge. A flabbergasted European visitor told of one small town where a local dignitary known as The General earned his title by his ability to train animals. Another observer found a fellow who was called The Judge because he was such a fine connoisseur of wines. Perhaps there was really nothing inconsistent in all this if one takes the point of view that in America democracy was so completely accepted that almost anyone could earn such "rank." Its achievement did not rest upon aristocratic blood, family origins, or privilege. Any village lad could make the grade by an earnest application of effort.

CORCORAN GALLERY OF ART

INDIANS OF THE PLAINS

The first trappers and settlers who entered the vast grasslands of North America lying between the Mississippi River and the Rocky Mountains came upon a civilization that was both new and startling to them. They found the world of the American Plains Indians, a hunting people who roamed the West much as the nomads roamed the desert. Their camps were moved seasonally, sometimes to escape hostile neighbors, but more often to follow the great herds of buffalo that supplied them with their meat for food, skins for clothing, and bones to be made into tools and weapons. Living as they did in land where the open space was almost without limitation, the plains people developed highly individual religious beliefs that helped them to cope with their great, lonely world. They conquered the physical problems and the dangers involved in traveling vast distances by becoming accomplished horsemen and warriors without peer. When the white man began to settle in the West, the old life on the plains was doomed. The buffalo was new and exciting game for hunters from the East, and extinction of the herds meant starvation for the Indians. Most important of all, the life of a wandering people could not be limited by the boundaries of farmers and ranchers. With all the fury and skill at their command, the plains tribes fought the advance of the frontier in the 19th century, retreating step by step, until, in the end, they were defeated by the superior number and weapons of the white man, and their civilization was lost.

THE
WANDERING LIFE

A party of Sioux sets out for a new camp (above). Their possessions are loaded on their backs or dragged on travois, the carriers made of poles that are hitched to horses and dogs. Riding ahead of the column, scouting braves are on the lookout for enemies. Except for encampments during the harsh winter months, the Plains Indian tribes were always on the move.

A Sioux village or camp is seen at the right. The women are preparing hides outside their tepees. These paintings were made by George Catlin, who went to the plains in the 1830s to record Indian life.

BOTH: AMERICAN MUSEUM OF NATURAL HISTORY

THE BUFFALO HUNT

A buffalo hunter prepares to take aim. Often the Indians could not find a herd of buffalo, and then they had to live on the meat they had preserved either by pounding it into a pulp and mixing it with fat or by drying it in long thin strips in the sun.

WEST POINT MUSEUM

The brave above hunts in the deep of winter on snowshoes, aided by his dogs. The buffalo hunt was more difficult for the Indians without horses, for the great herds moved swiftly across the open plains.

The wily hunters below, disguised in wolf-skins, are stealing up on a herd of buffalo with their bows and arrows in hand. Because a man on foot usually could not outrun a buffalo, he had to outwit him.

COLLECTION OF C. R. SMITH

AMERICAN MUSEUM OF NATURAL HISTORY

BOTH: SMITHSONIAN INSTITUTION

CORCORAN GALLERY OF ART

TALK, TOYS, AND SPORT

Mandan Indian braves (above, left) meet to smoke and exchange stories. Their lodge, which had a domed, earthen roof, served as a home, storehouse, stable, and kennel.

Plains Indian children played with small toys like those above. The pinto pony, buffalo, and elk—as well as the brave— were familiar sights in their daily life.

Life was not all hunting and fighting for the young Indian braves. The Sioux at the left are playing the fast, rough Indian game that the French named lacrosse.

503

ARTISTS OF THE PLAINS

An Indian Horse Dance.

YALE UNIVERSITY LIBRARY

OKLAHOMA HISTORICAL SOCIETY

In the Apache skin painting above, a ceremony is performed around a campfire in recognition of a girl's puberty. The dancers are girls, women, and medicine men.

An Indian artist did the stylized picture (opposite) of a ritual horse dance performed by the plains people. The rider shown full-face wears a buffalo mask.

The Sioux medicine shield at the right is decorated with a staring buffalo head. The Plains Indians had exceptional natural ability as artists and craftsmen.

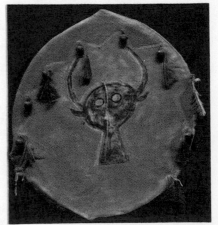

FLEMING MUSEUM, UNIVERSITY OF VERMONT

All of the Plains Indians followed ancient laws and ceremonies. At the tribal powwow above, the chief, in accordance with the custom of his people, will ask the advice of the tribal elders on a matter of importance to the whole tribe.

The Mandan below, standing in the center of a lodge roof, is invoking the aid of the gods in bringing rain for the crops of his tribe. The rain-making ritual was one of the most important magic rites practiced by the people of the plains.

SMITHSONIAN INSTITUTION

ANCIENT WAYS

WALTERS ART GALLERY, © 1951 UNIVERSITY OF OKLAHOMA PRESS

BOTH: AMERICAN MUSEUM OF NATURAL HISTORY

The Blackfoot woman above wears a head-dress for the Sun Dance ritual practiced by most Plains Indians. The participants evoked mystical visions while swaying, shuffling, and, sometimes, practicing forms of self-torture. The medicine man at the left, also a member of the Blackfoot tribe, wore his headdress while attempting to cure injuries and illnesses with ancient chants, ceremonies, and potions.

OVERLEAF: Men of the Mandan Bull Society do their frenzied ritual dance in an attempt to draw the great buffalo herds closer to their village. Mandan women also had an organization for this purpose.

YALE UNIVERSITY LIBRARY

CHAPTER 18

OPENING OF THE WEST

The Lewis and Clark expedition, sponsored by Jefferson, was the most important official examination of the high plains and the Northwest before the War of 1812. The President's secretary, Captain Meriwether Lewis, had been instructed to "explore the Missouri River, and such principal streams of it as, by its course and communication with the waters of the Pacific Ocean . . . may offer the most direct and practicable water communication across the continent, for the purposes of commerce." Captain William Clark, the younger brother of famed George Rogers Clark, was invited to share the command of the exploring party.

Amid rumors that there were prehistoric mammoths wandering around the unknown region, and that somewhere in its wilds was a mountain of rock salt, 80 by 45 miles in extent, the two captains set out. The date was May 14, 1804. Their point of departure was the mouth of the Wood River, just across the Mississippi from

Ready with rifles to attack, an Indian war party watches a wagon train, heading west, as it passes through its territory.

LINDLEY AND CHARLES EBERSTADT COLLECTION OF WESTERN PAINTINGS

the entrance of the Missouri River. After toiling up the Missouri all summer, the group wintered near the Mandan villages in the center of modern North Dakota. Resuming their journey in the spring of 1805, the men worked their way along the Missouri to its source and then crossed the mountains of western Montana and Idaho. Picking up a tributary of the Columbia River, they continued westward until they reached the Pacific Ocean, where they stayed until spring. Starting back early in 1806, they made the return journey safely, arriving at St. Louis in late September.

The long, hazardous trip excited the imagination of the American people and raised their interest in the West. Lewis and Clark brought back much new information, including the knowledge that the continent was wider than originally supposed. More specifically, they learned a good deal about river drainages and mountain barriers. They ended speculation that an easy coast-to-coast route existed via the Missouri-Columbia River systems, and their reports of the climate, the animals and birds, the trees and plants, and the natives of the West—though not

HISTORICAL SOCIETY OF MONTANA

immediately published—were made available to men of science.

The drama of the Lewis and Clark venture so occupied the public's attention that other significant explorations of the West during the same period went almost unnoticed. In 1804, as Lewis and Clark ascended the Missouri, a group of adventurers, led by William Dunbar and a Philadelphia chemist named Dr. George Hunter, moved up the Red River. The presence of hostile Spanish troops discouraged them, but they reached and explored the Washita River before they turned back. The next spring, Thomas Freeman, accompanied by a scientist, an army captain, and 19 men, again attempted to trace the Red River to its source. They examined it for some 600 miles, but also ran into Spanish opposition and withdrew.

The best known of those who explored the Central and Western plains were Lieutenant Zebulon Montgomery Pike and Major Stephen H. Long. In the summer of 1806, Pike crossed the plains to the Rocky Mountains, where he saw the peak that today bears his name. The next spring he examined the Royal Gorge of the Arkansas River and ventured into the San Luis Valley to the west. He moved too far south and was picked up by

BOTH: INDEPENDENCE NATIONAL HISTORICAL PARK, PHILADELPHIA

William Clark   *Meriwether Lewis*

Three boats and 43 persons headed up the Missouri from St. Louis on May 14, 1804, as Lewis and Clark began their exploration of the land bought from France in the Louisiana Purchase. The party met a band of friendly Flathead Indians at Ross's Hole, Montana, on September 4, 1805. The two explorers are seen at the far right.

Spanish soldiers, who charged him with trespassing. After a time in custody in Chihuahua, Mexico, where he was relieved of his notes and maps, he was escorted back to the United States border and handed over to American authorities. Fortunately he remembered enough of what he had seen to make a useful report of his travels.

In 1820, Major Long covered much the same ground, with the exception of the side trip into Spanish territory. With a handful of soldiers, he traveled to the Colorado Rockies, where he, too, found a peak to bear his name. Neither Pike nor Long made any startling discoveries, but they added to

the growing body of knowledge about the Western plains. Long is best remembered for the report of one of his associates who said the country they crossed on their way to the mountains was "almost wholly unfit for cultivation." Out of that and similar writings came the concept of the Great American Desert—a general belief that the country west of the Mississippi could not support a farming population. It held back further popular interest in the area for many years.

Some two decades later, a youthful officer named John C. Fremont resumed government explorations of the West. In 1842, guided by Kit Carson

513

and other trappers and hunters, he crossed the Continental Divide at South Pass, already discovered by fur traders, and then returned to Washington, D. C. The next year he again moved across South Pass and marched northward to Fort Hall, in modern Idaho. From there he explored the country along the Columbia River, after which he went south to Sutter's Fort (Sacramento) for the winter. Early in 1844 he was at Los Angeles, and from there he made his way east, to Santa Fe and St. Louis.

Explorers were not the only white men in the early West. Fur trappers, popularly called mountain men, roamed through the Rockies and the Western country, trapping beaver to send to the fur markets in St. Louis. A number of them, like Jedediah Smith, Jim Bridger, Tom Fitzpatrick, and the Sublette brothers, became well known to the public. But it was a businessman named John Jacob Astor, sitting in a New York office issuing orders in broken English, who was responsible for much of the new geographical knowledge that came from the fur frontier. Members of his Pacific Fur Company established themselves on the Columbia River in 1811, and though they were forced to abandon the area during the War of 1812, they brought back much information on the country between the Missouri and

The earliest eyewitness picture of Pawnee Indians, drawn by Samuel Seymour, was of an 1819 parley at Council Bluffs, Iowa.

514

the Pacific through which they had traveled or trapped. In 1822, Astor set up a western headquarters at St. Louis and sent men back up the Missouri River. His only real rival was the Rocky Mountain Fur Company, which provided violent opposition for a few years during the 1830s. Until the end of the beaver-pelt era, "King John" reigned supreme between St. Louis and Fort Benton, Montana.

Oregon fever

In the early 1820s, a member of Congress from Massachusetts advised his colleagues that "our natural boundary is the Pacific Ocean. The swelling tide of our population must

YALE UNIVERSITY LIBRARY

roll on until that mighty ocean interposes its waters, and limits our territorial empire." Another Congressman agreed, stating that the government was powerless to prevent the spread of population to the Pacific Coast. This notion of the helplessness of man or government to stem the mighty tide of Western expansion gave rise to the term "manifest destiny." Many who used it were not wholly sure of its meaning, but they imagined that somewhere in the great unknown, a divine hand was guiding the destiny of American growth and that the movement was irrepressible.

In the next two decades, the manifest-destiny virus spread across the land. Residents of the Mississippi Valley became especially excited over the prospect that their region would become the take-off point for the next step west and that great profits would result from supplying hardy Americans who were venturing into unsettled regions. The possibilities stimulated a tremendous burst of patriotism on the part of tradesmen, not to mention land speculators and farmers with produce to sell.

By the early 1840s there were settlements in Arkansas, Missouri, Iowa, and Minnesota. Beyond them, the Great American Desert still seemed unsuited for settlers. But across the plains was Oregon, now popularly ac-

HISTORICAL SOCIETY OF MONTANA

LIBRARY OF CONGRESS

NEW YORK CHAMBER OF COMMERCE

Jim Bridger   *John Charles Fremont*   *John Jacob Astor*

METROPOLITAN MUSEUM OF ART

cepted as a rich, fertile country. This huge territory lay west of the Rockies, north of parallel 42 (modern California's northern border) and south of parallel 54°40′ (Alaska's southern boundary). At one time, four nations claimed it—Spain, Russia, Great Britain, and the United States. In 1819, Spain relinquished her claim, and a few years later Russia followed, withdrawing to the 54°40′ parallel.

The two remaining claimants, the United States and Great Britain, were unable to agree upon an equitable division of the territory so, in 1818, they decided to hold it jointly. This was satisfactory when the only inhabitants were fur traders and Indians. But when American farmers began to talk of migrating to the new promised land,

Indians make their camp at the base of the towering Fremont Peak, named after the explorer who scaled it in 1842 on his expedition in Wyoming's Wind River Range.

as they did in the early 1840s, trouble arose.

What were the forces generating this new westward impulse? The common man was moved by favorable reports about Oregon from travelers, explorers, and missionaries and by a desire to better his economic condition. For generations the frontiersmen had believed that opportunities were greater just a little farther west, and the belief generally had proved to be sound. Now added to the personal incentive was the national eagerness to grow larger. The two elements combined to make an example of manifest destiny.

From a political standpoint, many American leaders encouraged the settlement of Oregon. It would "force the issue" with Great Britain and secure the region for the United States. The notion was proclaimed loudly by such Senators as Thomas Hart Benton of Missouri (the father-in-law of explorer John Fremont), who chafed at

517

WALTERS ART GALLERY. © 1951 UNIVERSITY OF OKLAHOMA PRESS

Chimney Rock in Nebraska was one of the great landmarks along the Oregon Trail. Alfred Jacob Miller painted it in 1837.

Britain's joint occupation of the distant territory. On one occasion, Benton urged his colleagues to "let the emigrants go on and carry their rifles. We want 30,000 rifles in the valley of the Oregon; they will make all quiet there."

Several events helped to stimulate the migration. The panic of 1837 caused many a farmer to hope things might be better on new land. Favorable reports from the Willamette Valley further roused this hope. Then, in 1841, a Senate bill proposed the construction of a line of forts up the Missouri River and across the mountains to the mouth of the Columbia. It also provided for Oregon land grants to male immigrants over 18 years of age. Although the bill was

lost in the House, such legislative activity suggested a deep interest on the part of the federal government in encouraging families to head west. People generally believed that next time the bill might pass.

The idea was enough to cause an epidemic of Oregon fever. In 1843, hundreds of prairie schooners moved out along the Platte River route, well known since the day of the fur traders, to mark off what was to be called the Oregon Trail. There were more wagons the next year. In 1845, some 3,000 men, women, and children migrated, almost doubling Oregon's population in a single travel season.

The occupation of Oregon by settlers made the question of its ownership urgent. The United States had repeatedly suggested dividing the territory at the 49th parallel, but the British government had held out for the Columbia River. The result had been a diplomatic stalemate, accompanied by American threats that now grew in intensity.

Texas—three times refused

Oregon was not the only land coveted by American farmers. The panic of 1819 made a good many farmers anxious to leave the Mississippi Valley and put their troubles and debts behind them. Spanish Texas looked attractive. In 1821, Moses Austin obtained a land grant from the defunct government of New Spain, but died before he could carry out his plan of colonization. His son Stephen carried

COLLECTION OF CLAUDE J. RANNEY

518

on and in 1822 received confirmation of his father's grant from the newly independent Mexican government. By 1825, young Austin's colony in Texas had a population of some 1,400 whites and over 400 slaves.

The American government was also interested in Texas. In August, 1829, President Jackson tried to buy it from Mexico for $5,000,000, but was turned down. Continued talk about acquiring the territory gradually aroused Mexican suspicions and made life hard for the colonists who had settled there. In time, the Mexican government began to pass restrictive legislation, limiting the number of American settlers in the area.

The climax came in March, 1836, when the Texans, led by Sam Houston, declared their independence. Prospects turned dark after the Texas garrison at the Alamo was wiped out, but on April 21, Houston and his volunteers defeated the Mexicans along the San Jacinto River and captured their leader, Santa Anna.

Although the now-independent Texans objected strenuously to outside control—from Mexico or any other authority—many of them wanted annexation by the United States. Sup-

A group of tenderfoot immigrants to the West, camped down for the night, sit and listen intently to the veteran trapper as he tries to explain what lies ahead.

posedly this was exactly what the federal government had wanted also, as it had repeatedly tried to buy Texas from Mexico. But Mexico did not recognize Texas' independence, and Andrew Jackson now became hesitant, concerned that annexation might split his party as well as involve the country in war. His successor, Martin Van Buren, adopted the same policy, and in the fall of 1838, the Texans, with feelings hurt, withdrew their application for annexation, asserting they no longer wanted to be in the Union.

The pique lasted only a few years. By 1843, Santa Anna was again threatening war against the Texans, and Great Britain, presuming to use its influence to prevent a conflict, showed an interest in the matter that worried the American State Department. President John Tyler, who had succeeded to office in 1841 at the death of William Henry Harrison, renewed negotiations with Texas for annexation.

Early in April, 1844, an annexation treaty was finally signed and sent to the Senate for ratification. Then another road block appeared. John C. Calhoun, a leader of Southern proslavery forces, was the new Secretary of State. When he presented the treaty on a sectional basis, suggesting that the inclusion of Texas in the Union was necessary to maintain the South's "peculiar institution," there was a violent reaction. As Marquis James wrote, "Had he turned loose a wildcat amid that decorous company, the result would have been much the same."

The proposal was soundly rejected.

Sam Houston, once again the Texas President, had warned his old friend Andrew Jackson that another rebuff to his people would be serious. He compared Texas to a bride "adorned for her espousals" and predicted that if "she should be rejected, her mortification would be indescribable." As this was the third time the bride-to-be had said yes, such a sentiment was understandable. But now the Senate had once more left the bride standing at the altar. It appeared as if only a miracle could save the romance.

The politics of expansion

The failure of the federal government's courtship of Texas threw the matter into the hands of the electorate. Not long after the Senate's action, both political parties assembled to nominate candidates for the election of 1844. Jackson, old and ailing but still the titular head of his party, had not lost his yearning for possession of Texas. Passing over a surprised Martin Van Buren, who had declared himself against annexation, Old Hickory came out for the relatively unknown James K. Polk. The Whigs, who did not plan to make the Texas question an election issue, nominated Henry Clay, an annexation opponent. They were confident that their candidate, celebrated as he was, would have little trouble beating the Democratic unknown from Tennessee.

Polk, the dark horse, used an old but effective device—a catchy cam-

LIBRARY OF CONGRESS   TEXAS MEMORIAL MUSEUM   MUSEUM OF HISTORY, CHAPULTEPEC CASTLE

Sam Houston   *Stephen Austin*   *Antonio Lopez de Santa Anna*

Austin brought the settlers into Texas in 1821, but it was not until Houston defeated Santa Anna at San Jacinto in 1836 that they won their freedom from Mexico.

paign slogan. Soon he and his followers had thousands of voters echoing "The Reoccupation of Oregon and the Reannexation of Texas." To this cry was added "54°40' or fight," meaning that the United States should take "All of Oregon or none," to quote another popular phrase.

The Democrats had enough political sagacity to capitalize upon a trend. Realizing that manifest destiny was running strong, they rode it to victory. "Harry of the West" managed to get only 105 electoral votes to Polk's 170. Apparently the voters approved enlarging the nation's territorial holdings. To Polk the mandate was clear.

The President-elect was to have part of his political harvest snatched away, however. The incumbent, John Tyler, wished to bring the Republic of Texas into the Union himself. He was faced by the difficult fact that the Senate had rejected the proposal and would surely repeat the insult if given a chance. There were just not enough pro-Texas votes for the necessary two-thirds. In December, 1844, Tyler proposed to Congress that a joint resolution, requiring only a simple majority of both Houses, be voted upon. The maneuver worked. The resolution passed the House easily, and squeaked by the Senate, 27 to 25. On March 1—three days before he left office—Tyler signed the resolution and at once notified Texas that it had been invited to become the 28th state.

When Polk was inaugurated, the annexation of Texas was practically complete, but another matter faced him. The campaign had raised threats of "54°40' or fight" over Oregon. Because this had been something of an election promise, he felt obliged to fulfill his party's campaign plank. He grumbled about it in his diary: "The truth is that in all this Oregon discussion in the Senate, too many Democratic Senators have been more concerned about the Presidential election in '48 than they have about settling Oregon, whether at 49° or 54°40'." But Polk was President, and the party leader. It was up to his administration to bring about some kind of settlement.

In 1846, the British indicated that they were ready to resolve the Oregon question if it could be done fairly. Polk wanted neither "54°40'" nor "fight," but how to compromise without losing face? At length he hit upon asking the Senate's advice. When that body agreed to the British suggestion of the 49th parallel, the President "reluctantly" accepted their opinion, assuming the attitude of being forced into the concession. On June 15, 1846, the Senate ratified the treaty, and the boundary was continued along parallel 49° from the Rockies to the Pacific Ocean. Oregon was "reoccupied."

Golden California

With Texas and Oregon in the fold, Americans now looked longingly at another part of the Pacific Coast—the Mexican province of California. Again Polk went along with public opinion, and when it was rumored that Great Britain had designs on that part of the continent, he believed it as quickly as the next man. Without hesitation he ordered a program of in-filtrating California by appointing Thomas O. Larkin as his secret agent to foment revolt among California Mexicans. At the same time, he made it clear to Mexico that he would pay as high as $40,000,000 for the province.

But Mexico showed no inclination to sell. In 1835, Andrew Jackson had tried without success to buy San Francisco Bay for half a million dollars; now, a decade later, Polk was faced with the same resistance in his attempt to buy all of California. Baring his frustration before Congress, he declared that the people of the North, American continent should have the right to decide their own destiny and promised protection from foreign interference to any independent state seeking entrance into the Union. He could not have made his position much clearer to those who were sewing their crude bear flags out beyond the towering Sierras.

On June 10, 1846, a group of settlers, dressed in greasy buckskins and wearing the mantle of manifest destiny, touched off the California bid for independence by stealing a band of General Jose Castro's horses. That they meant rebellion and not robbery was made plain a few days later when another group captured the prominent Mariano Vallejo and hauled him off to Sutter's Fort, despite his protestations that he favored peaceful acquisition of California by the Americans.

The uprising of the Californians was hastily improvised. Some of the Americans in the province attached themselves to the small command of John C. Fremont, who was in California on one of his expeditions of Western exploration. Other Americans made for Monterey and San Francisco, where United States ships provided naval aid. By July, the word had spread that the United States and Mexico were at war—a fact that permitted the Stars and Stripes to be raised over California localities with less embarrassment. Fremont's forces swept southward, meeting almost no resistance. On August 17, Commodore Robert F. Stockton announced at Los Angeles, "The flag of the United States is now flying from every commanding position in the Territory, and California is entirely free from Mexican domination." It was almost true. In September, a counterrevolution started in southern California that was not stamped out until mid-January, 1847.

A few weeks later, General Stephen Watts Kearny, who had marched his men across the Southwest to participate in the climax of hostilities, was formally installed as military governor. The manifest-destiny map makers had added another piece to their growing territorial mosaic and had pushed the westward-moving American frontier to the Pacific Ocean.

The Mexican War, formally terminated in February, 1848, gave final confirmation to the acquisition of California. Just a few days before the

A supply train, moving slowly across the desert to bring provisions to settlers who are farther west, is put into desperate flight by an Indian attack.

Treaty of Guadalupe Hidalgo was signed, an event occurred in the foothills of central California that would have made the Mexican signatories groan with dismay had they known of it. One of John Sutter's employees, James Marshall, found gold on the south fork of the American River while building a sawmill. This brought gold seekers from everywhere, and the human avalanche upon California was so great that the region was catapulted into statehood almost overnight. Bypassing the usual territorial stage of initiation, it entered the fraternity of states as part of the Compromise of 1850.

The Great Medicine Road

The tramping feet of men and beasts, westward bound, hammered out trails that later became roads and finally highways. Among the more important were the Santa Fe Trail angling across Missouri, Kansas, and southeastern Colorado to the ancient Spanish town that gave the trail its name; the Smoky Hill Passage across Kansas to the Colorado mines; and the Great Medicine Road, as the Indians called it, between the Missouri River and the West. The Great Medicine Road had several names. The Oregon immigrants had moved over it—out along the Platte, across present Wyoming and southern Idaho, to the Columbia River. The Mormons had followed them, in a general way, swinging down along the Green River and past Jim Bridger's establishment on Black's

Fork en route to the Salt Lake Valley. Then the California Argonauts had come, retracing the Mormons' steps and striking out across the bleakness that lay west of Salt Lake City in the hope of reaching the watercourses of the Sierras alive. So the roadway had become the Oregon Trail, the California Trail, or just the Great Western Road.

After the pioneers came stage lines, wagon-freighting companies, then the Union Pacific and Central Pacific Railroads, and finally automobile highways US 30 and 40 overlaid by Interstate 80 and 70. But long before the days of the superhighway, this main route west was well known to Americans. There were highly romanticized accounts of the ordeals of making the journey. A familiar image of the Oregon Trail in its heyday is of white-topped prairie schooners tightly circled, tongue to tailgate, surrounded by galloping savages, howling and dealing out death with their government-issue rifles. The more common hazards were just as deadly but less dramatic. Cholera killed more immigrants than did the Indians. Sicknesses of all kinds, accidents, malnutrition, and thirst caused the greatest hardships. Once the road was fairly well established, however, the risks diminished, and it was only a matter of time and boredom between the Missouri River and a Western destination.

As travel increased, way stations grew in number along various routes, and from these sprang small, isolated

GILCREASE INSTITUTE, TULSA, OKLAHOMA

Fort Laramie, Wyoming, on the North Platte River, was a fur-trading post and rendezvous for trappers and Indians until 1849, when the army took it over.

communities. Some of the settlements became important and demanded better communication with "the States." One of them was the Mormon center in Salt Lake Valley. As early as 1850, Samuel Woodson of Independence, Missouri, received a contract to carry the mail to the Mormons. He agreed to establish a monthly service across 1,200 miles of parched wilderness for approximately $20,000 a year. Up the Platte River route, past Fort Kearny, Nebraska, beyond Fort Laramie, to Jim Bridger's outpost went the mail-

bags. From there to Salt Lake City the going was easier. A few years later, when stagecoach service was established, the mail was delivered weekly and travel time was reduced from a month to 18 days.

The Overland Trail ran through the hunting grounds of the Plains Indians, and in 1849 the government responded to appeals for protection on the road by garrisoning Fort Laramie. It was not enough. To placate the Indians' growing restlessness, commissioners met with them at the fort in 1851. In

WALTERS ART GALLERY. © 1951 UNIVERSITY OF OKLAHOMA PRESS

The only known interior view of the original Fort Laramie, painted in 1837 by Alfred Jacob Miller, shows fur-trading Indians assembled in small groups.

this largest and most important meeting of its kind in the West, the tribes promised, in return for annuities and protection from the immigrants, not to molest travelers on the trail. But the council signalized the beginning of the end for the plains tribes. Before long, miners and settlers would overrun the countryside, paying no heed to Indian rights.

One of the outcomes of the Laramie Treaty was the establishment of a number of military posts along the great road. It resulted, in turn, in more traffic by men and vehicles sup-

plying the soldiers who guarded the route. And sometimes the blue-clad watchmen were overzealous. They took their duties so seriously that they brought on trouble where there was none before. A good example was the conduct of impulsive young Lieutenant J. L. Grattan, fresh from West Point and eager to make a name for himself at Fort Laramie. In the late summer of 1854, not long after the lieutenant had first come west, several bands of the Sioux were camped along the North Platte in the vicinity of the fort. On August 18, a cow wandered from a group of Scandinavian Mormons who were passing by, and the Indians killed it.

Several of the Sioux journeyed to Fort Laramie and reported the incident to the post commander, who requested Grattan to investigate. He set out at once with an intoxicated interpreter, a few mounted men, a wagonload of infantrymen, and two cannons, determined to bring back the offending Indian or Indians. At the Sioux camp there was a brief argument followed by threats, and then shooting. No white man survived the encounter, and the lieutenant's corpse, bristling like a porcupine with 24 arrows in it, was identified only with difficulty. An Indian agent who arrived at Fort Laramie shortly after the slaughter said that more reasonable conduct by the hotheaded army officer would have prevented bloodshed. In fact, he understood that the Indians had offered to pay for the cow, but the manner in which the negotiations were carried out had not given them the opportunity to make the offer to the lieutenant and his interpreter.

The Grattan massacre, as it was called, was followed by Indian raids on immigrant trains and freight convoys. These scattered attacks, together with a general sullenness among the Northern tribes, prompted the federal government to take punitive measures. Colonel William S. Harney moved out of Fort Kearny, Nebraska, in the summer of 1855 with 600 men and the loud announcement, "By God, I'm for battle—no peace." The colonel had his wish. There was battle, and there was no peace. The Indian wars were just beginning.

Meanwhile, traffic on the Medicine Road was becoming heavier. In May, 1857, some 2,500 federal troops under the command of Colonel Albert Sidney Johnston (who would, a few years later, die at Shiloh, wearing the Confederate gray) marched to Utah to quell rebellious Mormons. To the firm of Russell, Majors, and Wadell went contracts for supplying the soldiery. Here was a freighting organization with enough equipment of its own literally to supply an army: In 1858, it owned 3,500 wagons and 40,000 draft animals and had in its employ about 4,000 men. Horace Greeley, making a Western visit in 1859, was deeply impressed by the size of the company's operations: "Such acres of wagons! Such pyramids of extra axletrees! Such herds of oxen! Such regiments of drivers and other employees! No one who does not see can realize how vast a business this is, nor how immense is its outlay as well as its income. I presume this great firm has at this hour two millions of dollars invested in stock, mainly oxen, mules, and wagons." This was the scene at Leavenworth, Kansas. Although such a collection of transportation equipment was unusual, there were many smaller overland freighters at other starting points. Collectively they amounted to an enormous army, poised along the Missouri River, for

LIBRARY OF CONGRESS

Brigham Young

On April 9, 1847, the Mormon pioneers set out on the Oregon Trail to journey to the valley of the Great Salt Lake. Here they move into camp for the night, gather buffalo chips, and then light their fires.

the economic invasion of the West.

Trouble with the Mormons had stemmed from the Mexican War. When they moved into the Great Basin, they thought they were moving out of the United States, only to have the Treaty of Guadalupe Hidalgo thrust them back into it. By 1850, what is now Utah and most of Nevada, as well as some of present western Colorado and a bit of Wyoming, had become Utah Territory, with Brigham Young as governor. Difficulties between the governor and his appointed officials, especially the judiciary, led to a threat of civil violence in the new Zion. To halt the unrest, and perhaps to help take the nation's mind off the mounting slave crisis in the South, President Buchanan fired

CHURCH OF JESUS CHRIST OF LATTER-DAY SAINTS

Brigham Young and dispatched Colonel Johnston to Utah.

Winter overtook the slow-moving troops, obliging them to hole up at Fort Bridger until the weather moderated, and thus provided time for a peaceful settlement. In the summer of 1858, troops marched into Salt Lake

City peacefully, rebellious Mormons were pardoned, and the affair passed into history. Buchanan's bluff had cost the government about $15,000,000, much of which went into transport and supply for the expedition.

The Utah affair was concluded on the eve of the Civil War. Nearly six decades after the Louisiana Purchase, the trans-Mississippi West was still under examination by its new owners, and those who lived in it—both red and white—were restless and insecure. It was the postwar generation that settled the destiny of this vast part of the American Republic.

MAIN TEXT CONTINUES IN VOLUME 7

SOUTH DAKOTA STATE COLLEGE

530

Jedediah S. Smith:
Unsung Pathfinder of the West

A SPECIAL CONTRIBUTION BY
STEPHEN W. SEARS

At the age of 23, carrying a rifle and a Bible, Smith went into the Northwest Territory, and within five years was one of the best and most courageous explorers of unknown lands.

At the port of San Diego in December, 1826, Captain William Cunningham, master of the ship *Courier* out of Boston, recorded, "There has arrived at this place Capt. Jedediah Smith with a company of hunters, from St. Louis, on the Missouri. . . . Does it not seem incredible that a party of 14 men, depending entirely upon their rifles and traps for subsistence, will explore this vast continent, and call themselves happy when they can obtain the tail of a beaver to dine upon?"

The captain had witnessed the completion of the first overland journey to California, led by a fellow Yankee just 27 years old. This in itself was a solid achievement, but Jed Smith during a seven-year odyssey also found South Pass, the historic gateway to the Far West; discovered the arid vastness of the Great Basin; grasped the existence of the Sierra Nevada mountain barrier to California and made the initial crossing of that imposing range; and, finally, was the first white man to traverse virtually the entire length of America's Pacific coast, from southern California to the Columbia River in Oregon.

Jedediah Smith, not John C. Fremont, ought to be remembered today as the West's pathfinder. Yet his name never became impressed upon the American consciousness. Only recently has research by Western historians, particularly Maurice Sullivan and Dale Morgan, restored Jedediah Strong Smith to the first rank of America's explorers.

Arriving in St. Louis early in 1822 at the age of 23, Jed Smith sought a career in the mountains at precisely the moment when the long-restrained American assault on the Western fur trade burst loose. The depression following the War of 1812 had subsided, venture capital was again available, and the vicious Blackfeet Indians showed signs of being amenable.

Unfortunately, almost nothing was known of what lay on the far side of the Rocky Mountains. There was supposed to be a huge inland sea and a series of major westward-flowing rivers, especially the fabled Buenaventura. The headwaters of the Missouri and the far Northwest contained beaver in quantity. Why not the valleys of those mighty rivers of the West?

Jed Smith was later to write of his motives for going to St. Louis in 1822, "I started into the mountains with the determination of becoming a first-rate hunter, of making myself thoroughly acquainted with the character and habits of the Indians, of tracing out the sources of the Columbia River and following it to its mouth." To which he added, because he was a

While no likeness of Jedediah Smith exists, artist Harvey Dunn has captured the strength and spirit of the famous trapper and explorer.

When he was on the trail, Smith always took great precautions against the possibility of an Indian attack like the one that seems imminent in the painting by Alfred Jacob Miller.

New England Yankee at heart, "and of making the whole profitable to me."

Smith was born in 1799 of New England parents in what is now Bainbridge, New York. The family drifted westward to Erie County and later to Ohio's Western Reserve. Coming of age, Jedediah struck out for the frontier.

William H. Ashley, lieutenant governor of Missouri, was eager for a share in the fur-trade riches. In partnership with Andrew Henry, Ashley advertised for "Enterprising Young Men to ascend the river Missouri to its source." Smith quickly signed on and spent his first mountain winter with one of Henry's trapping parties high up the Missouri. In the spring, Henry dispatched him to tell Ashley to bring more horses.

Pulling up the Missouri with supplies, the party stopped to trade for horses with the Arikara Indians. Instead of trade, they got bullets. Smith and the shore party were pinned under a murderous fire, and before they could escape, 12 were dead and 11 wounded, two of them mortally.

Jed Smith hastened to Henry's outpost with the news, then returned to serve in a punitive military expedition against the Arikaras. Ashley's loss was considerable, but at least the Missouri artery was open again.

For the fall beaver hunt, Smith was given his first command. It was a party of exceptional quality, including Thomas Fitzpatrick, Jim Clyman, William Sublette, Thomas Eddie, and Edward Rose, all of whom became famous mountain men in their own right. They set off due west from the Missouri toward the Dakota Badlands and the Black Hills, breaking a new trail to the mountains. At one point, Smith was attacked by the mountain men's dreaded enemy, a grizzly bear. Clyman has left a description of the encounter: "Grissly did not hesitate a moment but sprang on the cap't. taking him by the head first pitc[h]ing [him]

sprawling on the earth . . . breaking several of his ribs and cutting his head badly. . . . The bear had taken nearly all his head in his capa[c]ious mouth close to his left eye on one side and clos to his right ear on the other and laid the skull bare to near the crown of the head. . . . One of his ears was torn from his head out to the outer rim."

Under Smith's cool direction, Clyman some-

WALTERS ART GALLERY, © 1951 UNIVERSITY OF OKLAHOMA PRESS

how stitched up the gaping wounds, even saving the ear.

The trappers plunged on into the Rockies, taking beaver and wintering with a tribe of friendly Crow Indians. On the spring hunt of 1824, they found a practical way west through the Divide via the wide gap of South Pass, and set about trapping the beaver-rich Green River Valley. Instructing Fitzpatrick to report these developments to Ashley, Smith and six of his men plunged deep into the mountains to the northwest.

Fitzpatrick's report of South Pass and the rich Green River Valley convinced Ashley to try and recoup his loss on the Missouri. He made the difficult march to the Green River, arriving in April, 1825, and set about trap-

COLLECTION OF EVERETT D. GRAFF

ping—but under a new system. His instructions read, "The place of deposite, as aforesaid, will be the place of rendavoze for all our parties on or before the 10th July next." Thus was born the effective rendezvous system that became the cornerstone of the American fur trade. No longer need the mountain man make the annual trek to civilization with his furs. Now supply caravans would come to him, buy his pelts, and sell to him in return—at astronomical prices—the supplies he needed to be self-sufficient the year round. The rendezvous became a wild carnival of gambling, races, monumental drunks, cavorting Indians, wenching, and storytelling, and the typical trapper

left it hung over and broke to return to his lonely beaver streams.

Smith was at that first rendezvous (quiet by later standards), where the logistics of the new practice were worked out. Andrew Henry had passed from the trade, and Smith became Ashley's new partner. A year later, he, William Sublette and David E. Jackson bought out Ashley. Jedediah Smith, after just four years in the mountains, became the senior partner of the firm that now dominated the American fur trade. He was 27.

The new partners realized that the beaver streams of the interior Rockies were becoming well enough known so that their productive

534

future was limited. But there were still those legendary rivers of the West hopefully thick with beaver, shown on the maps. Leaving Sublette and Jackson to handle matters in the mountains, Smith turned his face westward toward an unknown country.

In August of 1862 his party—the self-styled South West Expedition—rode along the Sevier River into what Smith called "a Country of Starvation—Sandy plains and Rocky Hills once in 20 30 or 40 m a little pond or Spring." Striking the Colorado at what is now Lake Mead, they followed it southward. On foot, their horses worn out, they fi-

At an annual rendezvous, trappers sold their furs to traders and bought supplies from them. Smith was at the first rendezvous, in 1825.

nally reached a haven in the Mojave villages not far from today's Needles, California. The expedition had so far found no beaver and no Buenaventura River coursing westward, and Smith determined to strike out for the coast.

It took two painful weeks to cross the blazing Mojave Desert, but at length they gained California's San Bernardino Valley, where they found a warm welcome at San Gabriel Mission. Smith's clerk, Harrison Rogers, described

535

MISSOURI HISTORICAL SOCIETY

This trapper, alone in wild country, is vulnerable, as Smith often was, to Indians and animals.

it: "Great feasting among the men. . . . I was introduced to the 2 Priests over a glass of good old whiskey—and found them to be very joval friendly gentlemen. . . . Plenty of good wine during supper, before the cloth was removed sigars was introduced. . . . Friendship and peace prevail with us and the Spanyards." In the spring of 1827, Smith headed into the San Joaquin Valley. He still sought the Buenaventura, hoping it would lead him to the summer rendezvous near Great Salt Lake.

He drove northward some 350 miles, but the looming presence of the Sierra Nevada formed a constant barrier to the east. There was no Buenaventura River. The 15-man party and its equipment was too cumbersome to cross the icy, snow-covered range. Leaving most of his men behind to trap the waters of the Stanislaus River, Smith set out with two companions, Robert Evans and Silas Gobel. They made the historic crossing of the Sierra, skirted Walker Lake, and struck out into central Nevada.

Smith's journal leaves a picture of the desert journey: "I could discover nothing but sandy plains or dry Rocky hills. . . . Worn down with hunger and fatigue and burning with thirst increased by the blazing sands . . . it then seemed possible and even probable we might perish in the desert unheard of and unpitied. . . . My dreams were not of Gold or ambitious honors but of my distant quiet home, of murmuring brooks, of Cooling Cascades."

Evans collapsed, and Smith and Gobel pressed on to find water. Smith returned with a kettle full. "Putting the kettle to his mouth, Evans did not take it away until he had drank 4 or 5 quarts and then asked me why I had not brought more."

At last they sighted Great Salt Lake and passed along its southern shore. To cross the flooded Jordan River, Smith cobbled together a raft for their belongings. Holding the towrope in his teeth, with Evans and Gobel hanging onto the raft, he swam them across. On July 3, 1827, having covered over 600 miles in six weeks, most of it on foot, the three men reached the rendezvous at Bear Lake, on the Utah-Idaho border. Smith laconically remarked that "my arrival caused a considerable bustle in camp, for myself and party had been given up as lost."

While Sublette and Jackson had done well, putting the new firm on a solid footing, Jed Smith was concerned about his own party stranded in California. Ten days after his arrival, he was headed southwest again with 18 men. Generally following the same route as the previous fall, they reached the Mojave Indian villages, but this time it was no haven.

The Mojaves had tangled painfully with trappers from Taos, and as the Americans crossed the Colorado, the vengeful Indians struck without warning. With eight survivors, Smith took refuge in a copse of cottonwoods, opened fire, and "the indians ran off like frightened sheep." Nonetheless, the situation was critical. All the horses and provisions, except 15 pounds of dried meat, were gone; to defend themselves, they had only their knives and five guns. There was no choice but to cross the desert on foot.

They reached the San Bernardino Valley in late August, and immediately moved north to rejoin the party left on the Stanislaus, arriving just two days ahead of the September 20 deadline Smith had set for his return.

Nothing had gone right so far, and Jed Smith's luck continued bad. Seeking supplies at San Jose Mission, his welcome was in sharp contrast to that described by Harrison Rogers the previous fall at San Gabriel. He was ordered to leave the territory by the military commandant at San Francisco. He sold his beaver skins and bought 250 horses and mules, which he intended to drive to the mountain rendezvous hundreds of miles to the east, where he might sell them at a 400% profit.

The previous year his California explorations had touched on the Sacramento River, and local rumor had it that its upper reaches angled northeast through the Sierra Nevada. Perhaps here was the Buenaventura at last—a navigable connection with the Columbia River system and a new route to the Rockies bypassing the deserts and salt plains. But the Sacramento was not the Buenaventura, and the northern California wilderness proved incredibly difficult to drive horses through. The heavy rains were constant and the geography confusing. Marauding Indians shot ar-

NEW YORK PUBLIC LIBRARY

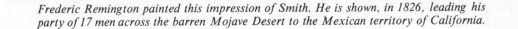

Frederic Remington painted this impression of Smith. He is shown, in 1826, leading his party of 17 men across the barren Mojave Desert to the Mexican territory of California.

rows into the herd, Smith was kicked by a mule and "hurt pretty bad," and Rogers was seriously mauled by a grizzly. Rogers' entry in his journal for May 22, 1828, reads, "Oh! God, may it please thee . . . to still guide, & protect us, through this wilderness of doubt & fear."

On July 14, the 19-man party was at the Umpqua River, halfway up the Oregon coast, and Smith and two men went ahead to scout. Two days previously they had disciplined a Kelawatset chief for stealing an axe, but now Rogers, left in charge of the camp, apparently felt secure because they were in well-ordered Hudson's Bay territory. He admitted a large number of Kelawatset tribesmen to the camp, and the Indians murderously avenged their chief's insult. Only one of the 16 men escaped. Smith, his two companions, and the lone survivor of the massacre managed to make their way on foot to the British Hudson's Bay Company base at Fort Vancouver on the Columbia, 100 miles to the north.

The destitute Smith was welcomed by Dr. John McLoughlin, who ruled the Columbia district for the company. McLoughlin immediately dispatched an expedition to reinforce discipline and try to recover the goods of his erstwhile competitor. Smith went with them and they gathered what they could—a few horses, part of the furs, a handful of guns and utensils, and, fortunately for history, the journals of Smith and Rogers. McLoughlin generously gave Smith a fair price for his horses and skins, and in return, Smith filled McLoughlin in on his extensive discoveries and made him a map that must have straightened out a prodigious amount of geographic confusion.

By August, 1829, Smith had rejoined his two partners in Montana, and during the next year they trapped with success the upper Missouri region and the Yellowstone and its tributaries. But Jed Smith had had his fill of the sudden death and desperate loneliness of the wilderness. At the rendezvous of 1830, he and his partners sold out, and Smith was able to return to St. Louis a moderately wealthy man, only eight years after first going there.

Knowing the West better than any man alive, he began to prepare his invaluable journals and maps for publication. But, fatefully, he invested in and joined a trading caravan to Santa Fe that left St. Louis in April, 1831. It should have been a routine journey, but the train went astray in the arid plain between the Arkansas and Cimarron Rivers and ran short of water. As he had done countless times before, Smith set out alone to find it, and the final tragedy overtook him.

The story was later pieced together from the accounts of Indian traders. Smith found water, but was trapped by a hostile Comanche war party. The violent, one-sided encounter was quickly over, but the Comanche chief died with him. The date was May 27, 1831, and Jed Smith was just 32 years old.

An anonymous eulogist wrote that "though he fell under the spears of the savages, and his body glutted the prairie wolf, and none can tell where his bones are bleaching, he must not be forgotten." But he *was* forgotten. Unaccountably, no one stepped forward to preserve or publish his work, and the journals and letters and maps were either destroyed by fire or simply dropped from sight.

His biographer, Dale Morgan, calls Smith "an authentic American hero," and it is a judgment hard to fault. Tall and wiry, blue-eyed, clean-shaven, of devout faith and high intelligence, Jed Smith was a breed apart from most of his wild-living, amoral compatriots. But he did have, in abundant measure, all of the mountain man's skills. He earned the grudging respect of his competitors and something much like awe among those who followed him. He had the sort of wide-ranging, inquiring mind that marks all great explorers. He even found time to send seeds gathered on his travels to a botanist friend.

The exploits of this remarkable man make it unlikely that such a heroic image will ever tarnish. This seems only fair, for Jedediah Smith, so quickly forgotten in his own time, certainly deserves to be remembered in ours.

Stephen Sears has been an editor of American Heritage *magazine and was a senior editor in the book division of American Heritage. He has written many books about American history.*

Volume 6
ENCYCLOPEDIC SECTION

The two-page reference guide below lists the entries by categories. The entries in this section supplement the subject matter covered in the text of this volume. A **cross-reference** (*see*) means that a separate entry appears elsewhere in this section. However, certain important persons and events mentioned here have individual entries in the Encyclopedic Section of another volume. Consult the Index in Volume 18.

AMERICAN PRESIDENTS AND STATESMEN

George Bancroft
Langdon Cheves
John C. Fremont
Robert Goodloe Harper

Joel Poinsett
James K. Polk
Robert F. Stockton
John Tyler
Abel Upshur

EXPANDING THE FRONTIER

William Henry Ashley
John Jacob Astor
Moses Austin
Stephen Austin
James P. Beckwourth
Black Hawk War
Daniel Boone
Sam Brannan
Jim Bridger
California Argonauts
Kit Carson
John Chapman
Distribution-Preemption Act of 1841
Tom Fitzpatrick
forty-niners
John C. Fremont
gold rush
Great Medicine Road

William S. Harney
Johnny Appleseed
Land Act of 1820
Thomas Larkin
Stephen H. Long
manifest destiny
Joaquin Murrieta
Oregon Trail
John L. O'Sullivan
Overland Trail
Plains Indians
Preemption Act of 1830
Preemption Act of 1841
Removal Act of 1830
Santa Fe Trail
Robert F. Stockton
John Sutter
Treaty of Fort Laramie

EXPLORERS

Daniel Boone
Jim Bridger
Kit Carson

Meriwether Lewis
Lewis and Clark expedition
Stephen H. Long

William Clark
James Clyman
William Dunbar
Tom Fitzpatrick
Thomas Freeman
John C. Fremont

Zebulon Montgomery Pike
William Rose
Sacagawea
Jedediah Smith
William Sublette
Charles Wilkes

FOREIGN RELATIONS

American Peace Society
Aroostook War
Clayton-Bulwer Treaty
William Ladd
Thomas Larkin
Liberia

manifest destiny
Matthew Calbraith Perry
Joel Poinsett
Robert F. Stockton
William Walker
Webster-Ashburton Treaty
Charles Wilkes

REFORM LEADERS AND MOVEMENTS

abolitionists
American Anti-Slavery Society
American Colonization Society
American Temperance Union
Timothy Shay Arthur
Henry Barnard
James G. Birney
Amelia Bloomer
Orestes Brownson
William Cullen Bryant
Dorothea Lynde Dix
Thomas Eddy
Elihu Embree
Charles G. Finney

William Lloyd Garrison
Robert Goodloe Harper
William Ladd
Liberia
Liberty Party
Benjamin Lundy
William Holmes McGuffey
Lucretia Mott
Theodore Parker
Elizabeth Cady Stanton
Temperance Movement
United States Temperance Union
Denmark Vesey
Washingtonians
Theodore Dwight Weld

THOUGHT AND CULTURE

Bronson Alcott
Timothy Shay Arthur
George Bancroft
Henry Barnard
Phineas T. Barnum
Albert Bierstadt
Orestes Brownson
William Cullen Bryant
George Catlin
James Fenimore Cooper
William Dunbar
Seth Eastman
Ralph Waldo Emerson
Edwin Forrest

Stephen Collins Foster
Margaret Fuller
Sarah Hale
Chester Harding
Charles Lesueur
Jenny Lind
William Holmes McGuffey
Alfred Jacob Miller
Samuel Francis Smith
Smithsonian Institution
Henry David Thoreau
Transcendentalism
John Greenleaf Whittier
Charles Wimar

UTOPIANS AND UTOPIAN COMMUNITIES

Brook Farm
Charles Lesueur
Mormons
New Harmony

John Humphrey Noyes
Oneida Community
Robert Owen
Joseph Smith
Brigham Young

A

ABOLITIONISTS. The term *abolitionists* refers to Americans who wanted an end to slavery, although they often differed on how to achieve that goal. Before the 1830s, most antislavery groups in the nation worked for gradual emancipation. Some tried to set up a colony of freed blacks in America, or like the **American Colonization Society** (*see*), a settlement in Africa. All were opposed to the extension of slavery in new states entering the Union. In the latter half of the 1820s, a strong religious revivalist movement, led by **Charles G. Finney** (*see*), swept much of the nation, and with it came a demand for social reforms. In 1831, **William Lloyd Garrison** (*see*) loudly demanded the immediate abolition of slavery, which he proclaimed a moral evil. Two years later, with Garrison's help, the first important national organization, the American Anti-Slavery Society, was founded in Philadelphia. The society established local chapters, circulated antislavery literature, and sent petitions to Congress. However, by the end of the 1830s, a serious disagreement over methods arose among abolitionists. Radicals such as Garrison refused to consider political action to achieve abolition. He later went so far as to publicly burn the Constitution. Moderates, on the other hand, formed the **Liberty Party** and ran **James G. Birney** (*see both*) for President in 1840 and 1844. Following Birney's defeats, many moderates then supported the Free Soil Party in the elections of 1848 and 1852 and finally, in 1854, backed the new Republican Party. Many historians believe that the uncompromising nature

WORCESTER ART MUSEUM

This dramatic abolitionist symbol appeared in Garrison's famous Liberator.

of the abolition movement made civil war the only possible solution to the slavery question.

ALCOTT, (Amos) Bronson (1799–1888). Alcott, a leading exponent of **Transcendentalism** (*see*), evolved what were then considered radical theories of education. Born in Connecticut, he had little formal education himself and early in his life was a peddler in Virginia and the Carolinas. In 1823, he returned to Connecticut and taught in various schools. He believed that children should learn by conversation and pleasant activities, as opposed to the strict educational methods then in practice. However, these ideas, coupled with Alcott's unorthodox religious views, prevented him from having a successful teaching career. In 1836, he moved to Concord, Massachusetts, where he met **Henry David Thoreau** and **Ralph Waldo Emerson** (*see both*) and became a leading member of the Transcendentalist movement there. In 1844, hoping to return to a simpler form of life, he founded a cooperative farming community near the village of Harvard. Although the experiment failed, Alcott was able to apply some of his educational

theories upon his return to Concord. He was appointed superintendent of the school system there in 1859 and instituted a number of reforms. His daughter, Louisa May Alcott (1832–1888), was the author of *Little Women* (1868) and many other books.

AMERICAN ANTI-SLAVERY SOCIETY. *See* **abolitionists.**

AMERICAN COLONIZATION SOCIETY. This society promoted the emigration of free blacks from America to Africa. It also purchased the freedom of many slaves so they could emigrate, too. The society was founded in 1816 by a Presbyterian minister, Robert Finley (1772–1817), and among its first members were two Presidents, James Madison (1751–1836) and James Monroe (1758–1831). The society, which established chapters in every state, provided funds to purchase land from the natives at Cape Mesurado on the west coast of Africa. The first permanent settlement was established there in 1822. The colony—at the suggestion of **Robert G. Harper** (*see*)—was named Liberia, and the settlement Monrovia, in honor of President Monroe. Until 1830, the society was especially popular with Southern and border-state residents who wanted to provide a homeland outside the United States for free blacks. Its efforts were hampered by attacks from, among others, radical **abolitionists** (*see*). Many abolitionists believed that the removal of free blacks and the example they provided would only serve to buttress slavery. The society also ran into an unwillingness on the part of free blacks to emigrate. It has been variously estimated that between 6,000 and 12,000 blacks had sailed for Liberia by the time of the Civil War. However, membership in the society dropped off sharply as war approached. After the war, the society functioned mainly as a trustee for Liberia, until the organization was dissolved in 1912.

AMERICAN PEACE SOCIETY. Founded in 1828 by **William Ladd** (*see*), the American Peace Society was dedicated to establishing a "Congress and High Court of Nations" to establish principles of international law and to arbitrate disputes between nations. It was made up of many state and local pacifist groups and was active in promoting legislation to ban all warfare. Although the society advocated the principle of nonresistance, it backed the Union during the Civil War and also supported the government during both World Wars. Throughout its history, the society published a periodical, *World Affairs*. The organization finally disbanded when the United Nations was established in 1945.

AMERICAN TEMPERANCE UNION. The **temperance movement** (*see*) was firmly launched with the founding of this union in 1826 by a group of 16 ministers and laymen in Boston. The organization was originally known as the American Society for the Promotion of Temperance. The reformers used religious and moral arguments to convince people to give up strong alcoholic beverages. The organization sent missionaries out to get people to sign temperance pledges. It also sponsored sermons and rallies and published periodicals devoted to temperance themes. By 1834, the society had become national in scope and had become known as the American Temperance Union. It boasted 5,000 branches, with a combined membership of 1,000,000 persons. At its annual convention in 1836, a proposal was made to ban the imbibing of even mildly alcoholic drinks—such as wine and malt liquor—which until that time had been considered harmless. This additional restriction was adopted, but by a narrow margin. As a result, many members quit the union rather than give up their daily glass of wine or malt brew.

AROOSTOOK WAR. This so-called war between the United States and Britain—which was brief, bloodless, and undeclared—occurred in 1839 over the boundary separating Maine from the Canadian province of New Brunswick. The boundary had been left undetermined by the Treaty of Paris, which officially ended the Revolutionary War in 1783. Soon after Maine became a state in 1820, its legislature, together with the Massachusetts legislature, made land grants to settlers along the Aroostook River, disregarding British claims to that area. When Canadian lumberjacks began to build a road there for lumbering operations, Rufus McIntire was appointed land agent, with authority to eject the Canadians. When he was arrested by the Canadians in February, 1839, Maine and New Brunswick called out their militias. Ten thousand Maine troops were sent into the disputed region, and Congress allocated $10,000,000 to raise an army of 50,000 men for possible war. To avoid any bloodshed, President Martin Van Buren (1782–1862) sent General Winfield Scott (1786–1866) to negotiate a truce between the lieutenant governor of New Brunswick and the governor of Maine. A truce was arranged in March, 1839. The dispute was referred to a boundary commission, whose conclusions were embodied in the **Webster-Ashburton Treaty** (*see*) in 1842.

ARTHUR, Timothy Shay (1809–1885). Arthur, a temperance man, wrote about 70 books of "moral instruction," including the highly popular *Ten Nights in a Barroom* (*see p. 490*). Born near Newburgh, New York, Arthur was such a poor student that his teacher recommended that he be dropped from school. He was apprenticed to a watchmaker, but poor eyesight forced him to abandon that trade. Arthur then became a clerk in Baltimore and went on to edit several local weeklies. He moved to Philadelphia in 1841 and published his first book—a group of temperance stories—the next year. In 1854, he wrote *Ten Nights in a Barroom*. The characters in this novella included a drunken father, his suffering wife and daughter, Gambler Green (who died horribly), and Frank Slade, son of the tavern owner, who killed his father in a drunken rage. The book, with its sensational plot and moral tone, was an immense success. No Sunday-school library was considered complete without a copy of it. All of Arthur's later books warned against immorality, gambling, and above all, drinking.

ASHLEY, William Henry (1778?–1838). Ashley was a leading explorer and one of the most successful fur traders in the West. He was born in Virginia and moved to present-day Missouri about 1804. There Ashley engaged in lead mining and the manufacture of gunpowder. In 1820, he became Missouri's first lieutenant governor and two years later was made commander of the state militia. That same year, he and Andrew Henry (1775?–1833) established the Rocky Mountain Fur Company. Their initial trading ventures ended in failure—on one trip, a keelboat and its $10,000 cargo sank, and on another, a band of Arikara Indians attacked the traders. However, Ashley's luck soon changed, and by 1828 he was a rich man. Working for him were **Jedediah Smith, William Sublette, Jim Bridger,** and **James P. Beckwourth** (*see all*). Ashley took personal charge of several remarkable expeditions, all as part of his fur-trading operation. In 1822, he explored the upper Missouri River region and in 1825 journeyed down the turbulent Green River, which he navigated in a buffalo-skin boat. He reached the vicinity of the Great Salt Lake in present-day Utah in 1826. That same year, Ashley sold his share in the company, but he continued to supply goods to his successors. He later represented Missouri in Congress, where he vigorously opposed any peacemaking with the Indians.

ASTOR, John Jacob (1763–1848). A fur trader, financier, and real-estate magnate, Astor became the richest man of his time in America. Born in Germany, he immigrated to New York City in 1784 and was apparently first employed by a furrier. Within two years, Astor opened his own fur business. He made frequent trading trips to the frontier and by 1800 was the nation's leading fur agent. He began to create a vast commercial empire by acquiring property in the city and by chartering, about 1800, a ship that made $50,000 for him in one trading venture to the Orient. After hearing about the successful **Lewis and Clark expedition** (*see*), Astor formed the American Fur Company in 1808 and the Pacific Fur Company in

1810, and he set up a central headquarters, situated at the mouth of the Columbia River, in present-day Oregon. The settlement, named Astoria, was founded in 1811 to serve as a trading port with China. However, the British wrested control of it at the outbreak of the War of 1812. Despite this loss, Astor profited from the war by lending money to the United States government and trading with the British throughout the conflict. Meanwhile, his real-estate holdings increased in value. The government later passed legislation enabling Astor to monopolize trade in the Mississippi and upper Missouri Valleys. He soon acquired a reputation for ruthlessness. His agents intimidated government officials and sold liquor to the Indians in order to obtain pelts. However, having failed to wipe out the rival Rocky Mountain Fur Company, Astor sold his fur interests in 1834. He spent the rest of his life managing his property. When he died, his estate was worth more than $20,000,000.

AUSTIN, Moses (1761–1821). Austin, a merchant and mine owner, began the colonization of Texas by American settlers. Born in Connecticut, Austin joined an importing company in 1783. After six years, he had established a branch office in Richmond, Virginia, and had acquired rich lead mines in the southwestern part of the state. He moved west into present-day Missouri in 1796 to acquire more mines. Although he was worth over $150,000 in 1812, Austin lost most of his fortune during the Panic of 1819. The following year, he again moved westward, this time to Texas, where he applied to the Spanish governor for permission to settle 300 families of colonists. The per-

mit was granted early in 1821, but Austin died before final arrangements for the colony were completed. His son, **Stephen Austin** (*see*), led the first settlers there in 1822.

AUSTIN, Stephen Fuller (1793–1836). Austin is credited with being the founder of Texas. His father, **Moses Austin** (*see*), had, prior to his death in 1821, received a land grant for the first settlement there. In order to carry out his father's colonization plans, young Austin visited Texas, then part of Spanish Mexico, to confirm the arrangements his father had made with the Spanish governor of Texas to settle 300 families in the territory. Early in 1822, he established the first legal American settlement in Texas, on the rich land between the Brazos and Colorado Rivers. Because Mexico had gained its independence from Spain in the fall of 1821, Austin traveled to Mexico City to petition

BERRY-HILL GALLERIES, INC.

Stephen Austin

the new government for permission to remain in Texas. After his land grant was again confirmed in 1823, Austin ruled the colony with almost dictatorial powers until the organization of a constitutional government five years later. During this time, he created a land-grant system for new colonists, promoted the establishment of industries and schools, and fought off the Indians. Persons from all over America responded to the lure of cheap land, and the colony grew rapidly. In 1833, Austin went again to Mexico City, this time to negotiate a separate status for Texas, which was then part of the combined Mexican state of Coahuila and Texas. Austin considered himself a Mexican citizen, but he feared that his Texans would revolt rather than remain joined to Coahuila. His views, however, offended Mexican leaders, and he was jailed for two years. After his return to Texas in 1835, the colonists revolted against Mexico. Austin served briefly as commander of the Texas forces until he was replaced by Samuel Houston (1793–1863) that December. He then went to Washington to secure supplies for his soldiers. After the Texans won their independence in 1836, Austin served as secretary of state for the new republic until his death later that year. Austin, the state capital, is named in his honor.

B

BANCROFT, George (1800–1891). Both a statesman and a scholar, Bancroft throughout his career was either helping to shape American history or writing about it. Born in Massachusetts, Bancroft entered Harvard at the age of 13, and after graduate study in

LIBRARY OF CONGRESS: MATHEW BRADY COLLECTION

George Bancroft

Germany, published in 1834 the first volume of his monumental 10-volume *History of the United States*. Although only three volumes were completed by 1840, Bancroft was immediately recognized as one of the most distinguished authors of his day. At the same time, he worked for the Democratic Party in Massachusetts and was rewarded in 1837 by being appointed collector of the Port of Boston. Bancroft became a supporter of **James K. Polk** (*see*), and when Polk was elected President, he was appointed Secretary of the Navy (1845–1846). In this post, Bancroft signed the order directing General Zachary Taylor (1784–1850) to cross into Texas in 1845, an act that led to the Mexican War. He was also instrumental in founding the Naval Academy at Annapolis, Maryland. In 1846, Polk chose Bancroft to be minister to Britain. While he was there, the British government allowed him to study public and private records and archives. With the use of such information, Bancroft, on his return to America in 1849, spent the next 18 years con-

tinuing to work on his *History,* publishing six additional volumes from 1852 to 1866. A year later, he became the United States minister to Prussia and later held several other ministerial posts abroad until his retirement in 1874. That same year, he published the 10th and final volume of his *History.* His last 17 years were divided between Newport, Rhode Island, and Washington, D.C., where, a familiar figure with flowing white beard, he continued the reading and study he had enjoyed throughout his life.

BARNARD, Henry (1811–1900). One of America's foremost educators, Barnard was the first United States Commissioner of Education. He pioneered in promoting the regular inspection of schools, parent-teacher meetings, school libraries, and new methods of examination. Born in Connecticut, Barnard graduated from Yale in 1830. For the next five years, he taught school and studied law. He was admitted to the bar in 1835. Two years later, he was elected to the Connecticut legislature, where he had a law enacted "to provide for the better supervision of the common schools." The law set up a state education commission, and Barnard became its secretary. In 1843, he was appointed the first public school commissioner of Rhode Island and helped to establish the Rhode Island Institute of Instruction in 1845. He returned to Connecticut in 1849 as superintendent of common schools. Through his writing and lectures, Barnard's views on public education had become widely known in this country and Europe. After serving as chancellor of the University of Wisconsin (1858–1860) and president of St. John's College in Annapolis,

Maryland (1866–1867), Barnard was appointed the first federal Commissioner of Education in 1867. He held the post for three years, preparing many reports on education both in the United States and abroad. His 32-volume *American Journal of Education,* which he personally financed and edited between 1855 and 1882, became an important encyclopedia of educational theories from many nations.

BARNUM, Phineas T. (1810–1891). Called America's greatest showman, Barnum is best remembered for his circus, The Greatest Show on Earth. Although few of Barnum's entertainment ideas were original, he pioneered in producing acts and exhibitions of varied, sometimes bizarre, interest and promoted his attractions with extravagant advertising and publicity stunts. Barnum was born in Bethel, Connecticut, and worked until he was 25 at odd jobs, running a store,

tending bar, and even managing an abolitionist paper. However, he disliked manual labor and resolved to earn a living with his wits. His show-business career began in 1835, when he "discovered" an old Negro woman, Joice Heth, who claimed to be more than 160 years old and the former nurse of George Washington (1732–1799). Barnum put the woman on exhibit in New York, and the paying public flocked to see her. When the fraud was later exposed— Joice was only about 80—Barnum was unfazed. "There's a sucker born every minute" was his motto. In 1842, he opened the American Museum in New York, a popular entertainment center that not only featured a "Feejee" mermaid, a woolly horse, and Tom Thumb, the famous midget, but also contained a theater and a menagerie. Barnum amazed the entertainment world in 1850 by persuading **Jenny Lind** (*see*), the celebrated Swedish soprano, to tour the United States under his sponsorship. In England

in 1858, he lectured on "The Science of Money Making and the Philosophy of Humbug." Barnum opened his circus in Brooklyn in 1871. Among the marvels it featured were wild men from Borneo, a plastic man, and other freaks. The flamboyant Barnum merged his show with that of his chief rival, James A. Bailey (1847–1906), in 1881. One of their major attractions was Jumbo, an African elephant that Barnum called "The Only Mastodon on Earth."

BECKWOURTH, James P. (1798–1867?). Beckwourth was a noted mountain man in the American West. Born in Virginia, Beckwourth, a mulatto, joined an expedition organized by **William H. Ashley** (*see*) in 1823, apparently as a groom, and the following winter he accompanied Ashley to the Rocky Mountains. He subsequently worked for the American Fur Company (*see* **John Jacob Astor**). For six years prior to 1833, Beckwourth lived among the Crow Indians as a member of their tribe. He adopted their customs and married a Crow woman. Beckwourth's later career took him to California and present-day Colorado, where he died. Much of what is known about him is based on an autobiography, *Life and Adventures of James P. Beckwourth, Mountaineer, Scout, and Pioneer and Chief of the Crow Nation of Indians* (1856), which Beckwourth dictated. It is considered exaggerated. Beckwourth claimed, for example, that he was a Crow chief and related numerous tall tales about his life among the Indians.

BIERSTADT, Albert (1830–1902). A landscape artist, Bierstadt was known for his panoramic vistas of the West. In 1858, the German-born painter accompanied a sur-

MUSEUM OF THE CITY OF NEW YORK

P. T. Barnum doffs his hat to royalty in an appearance at a London theater.

veying expedition for a wagon route to the West, sketching the scenery along the way. These drawings served as models for the paintings he later did (*see front endsheet*) at his New York studio. Although his huge canvases were highly popular, Bierstadt's fame rests on his earlier, small-scale landscapes, which are known for their charm and spontaneity. In his later years, Bierstadt also became known for his illustrations of the wild animals of North America.

BIRNEY, James Gillespie (1792–1857). Although a Kentucky-born slave owner, Birney became the nation's leading spokesman for political action to free the slaves (*see* **abolitionists**). Birney began his law practice in 1814 and moved to Alabama two years later. In the mid-1820s, he publicly supported the restriction of slavery and of the sale of slaves between states. He also believed in the gradual emancipation of the slaves and supported the attempt by the **American Colonization Society** (*see*) to found an African settlement for free blacks. A visit to New York and New England in 1829 convinced him of the superiority of free economic and social institutions, and by 1834 Birney, who had returned to Kentucky, adopted an aggressive abolitionist position. He freed his six slaves and subsequently became active in various antislavery societies. By 1837, Birney had become America's strongest advocate of constitutional and political action in the fight against slavery. His views differed from those of many other abolitionists, especially **William Lloyd Garrison** (*see*). Garrison, for one, regarded the antislavery movement purely as a moral crusade and refused to take part in

political efforts for emancipation. Birney became the leader of a group of politically oriented abolitionists who formed the **Liberty Party** (*see*) in 1840. He ran unsuccessfully as that party's Presidential candidate in the elections of 1840 and 1844. In the summer of 1845, Birney retired from politics after falling from a horse, an accident that left him partly paralyzed.

BLACK HAWK WAR. This conflict between Indians and settlers in Illinois and present-day Wisconsin in 1832 was the climax of land disputes dating back to 1804. At that time, the Sauk and Fox Indian tribes ceded to the United States 50,000,000 acres of land, including large parts of what are now Wisconsin, Missouri, and northwestern Illinois. However, Chief Black Hawk (1767–1838), one of the Sauk tribal leaders, believed that his people had been cheated and refused to leave the land. Years of raids and violent incidents followed, until, in 1831, the whites finally drove Black Hawk across the Mississippi River into present-day Iowa. Early the next year, Black Hawk and about 400 warriors and their families returned to Illinois with the intention of settling and raising corn. General Henry Atkinson (1782–1842) raised a force of volunteers and ordered Black Hawk to go back to Iowa. Badly outnumbered, Black Hawk made peace overtures. However, one of his envoys was murdered, and the angry chief attacked and defeated a superior force of whites and then raided settlements. Atkinson pursued him with a force of 1,300 men and on August 3, 1832, massacred Black Hawk's followers at the Bad Axe River in Wisconsin. The Indians were subsequently forced to cede

their land in Iowa to the United States. The government paid them 14¢ an acre for it.

BLOOMER, Amelia Jenks (1818–1894). A noted 19th-century social reformer, Mrs. Bloomer is best remembered for the dress reform she first advocated in 1851. The costume consisted of a jacket with narrow sleeves, a short skirt, and Turkish-style pantaloons (*see p. 493*). Even though she wore the costume herself for several years, it was so ridiculed on the stage and in the comic papers of the time that other women never copied her. However, the pantaloons became standard for women's athletic wear and were known as bloomers. Amelia Jenks, whose formal education had been limited to a few terms in public school, was a governess and tutor to three small children in a private family before she married Dexter C. Bloomer of Seneca Falls, New York, in 1840. He was a Quaker and the editor of the weekly *Seneca County Courier*. Soon Mrs. Bloomer began writing anonymous articles on social, political, and moral topics for her husband's paper. Then, in 1848, she heard **Lucretia Mott** and **Elizabeth Cady Stanton** (*see both*) speak at the first public meeting for women's rights, which was held at Seneca Falls. The next year, Mrs. Bloomer started her own paper, *The Lily*, which carried articles on education, temperance, abolition, and marriage laws as well as women's rights. By 1853, the subscribers numbered 4,000. When she moved with her husband to Council Bluffs, Iowa, in 1855, Mrs. Bloomer stopped publishing *The Lily* because there was no railroad nearby for mailing it. However, she continued to write and lecture.

STATE DEPARTMENT OF ARCHIVES AND HISTORY, RALEIGH, NORTH CAROLINA

Daniel Boone

BOONE, Daniel (1734–1820). One of America's most famous frontier heroes, Boone pioneered in the settlement of Kentucky. He was born near Reading, Pennsylvania, to a family of Quakers. He received little formal education but possessed a shrewd native intelligence and became an expert rifleman and scout. After moving to North Carolina in 1750, Boone took hunting and fur-trading trips into Virginia and present-day Tennessee. In 1755, he was a wagoner in the unsuccessful British expedition against the French at Fort Duquesne, barely escaping with his life. Boone began explorations of Kentucky, then part of Virginia, in 1767. He founded Boonesborough in 1775 after blazing a trail through the Cumberland Gap that became known as the Wilderness Road. It later was a major route for settlers heading west. In 1778, Boone was captured by the Shawnee Indians and held prisoner for five months before escaping. Boone lost his extensive landholdings in Kentucky because his claims had not been filed properly. He moved to what is now West Virginia in 1789, and 10 years later he finally settled in the Ozark region of present-day Missouri.

One of Boone's exploits was later fictionalized by James Fenimore Cooper in *The Last of the Mohicans* (1826).

BRANNAN, Samuel ("Sam") (1819–1899). Brannan, a newspaper publisher, rushed to San Francisco with the news of the gold strike at Sutter's mill in California in 1848 and later became a wealthy property owner. Brannan had grown up in Ohio and traveled as a printer throughout the states until he settled in New York in 1842. That same year, he became a Mormon. In 1846, Brannan led a group of 238 Mormons that went by ship to settle in California. He published the first newspaper in San Francisco, the *California Star,* in 1847. He then opened a store in Sutter's Fort, a few miles from Sutter's mill, near Sacramento. On learning that gold had been found, Brannan reportedly "bolted into San Francisco," hatless and dirty from his trip, and ran through the town square, shouting, "Gold! Gold from the American River!" The news spread rapidly, leading to the **gold rush** (*see*). Brannan closed his store in 1849 and made clever real-estate investments in Sacramento and San Francisco. In 1851, he served briefly as the head of the vigilante committee that maintained law and order in San Francisco during the height of the gold rush. For the next 10 years, Brannan busied himself establishing, among other things, banks and railroad companies and also contributed large sums to charity. However, he took to drink and by the time of his death was penniless.

BRIDGER, James ("Jim") (1804–1881). A blacksmith by trade, Bridger answered an adver-

tisement in a St. Louis newspaper in 1822 requesting young men for a fur-trapping expedition. He thus began a career that led him to become one of the most celebrated trappers and frontier scouts in the West. After going on the expedition up the Missouri River with **William H. Ashley** (*see*), he accompanied **Jedediah Smith** (*see*) on a journey to the Big Horn Mountains in what is now northern Wyoming, and in 1824 he was the first white man to see the Great Salt Lake. Bridger worked for more than 20 years as a trapper, becoming well acquainted with the American West. In 1843, he established Fort Bridger on the **Oregon Trail** (*see*) in southwestern Wyoming, where his knowledge of the area was invaluable to settlers. Forced out of the post 10 years later by Mormons who wanted to monopolize trade with the newcomers, Bridger became a government scout and guided General Albert Sidney Johnston (1803–1862) in the invasion of Utah

NORTHERN NATURAL GAS CO. COLLECTION, JOSLYN ART MUSEUM, OMAHA, NEBRASKA

Alfred Miller painted frontiersman Jim Bridger wearing a suit of armor.

(1857–1858). He served on other expeditions until he retired in 1868.

BROOK FARM. Officially known as the Brook Farm Institute of Agriculture and Education, Brook Farm in West Roxbury, Massachusetts, flourished as an experiment in cooperative communal living from 1841 to 1847. It became a center of intellectual life in the nation but failed as a practical community because of poor soil and the lack of experienced farmers. Brook Farm was founded and directed by George Ripley (1802–1880), the Transcendentalist philosopher (*see* **Transcendentalism**), and was a self-supporting community of "plain living and high thinking." Its members, each of whom owned stock in the institute, shared in doing the chores on the farm and spent the rest of

their time writing and holding discussions. Each was paid $1 a day for whatever he had done, whether manual or intellectual work. The institute was governed by a board of directors that included, for a brief period, the author Nathaniel Hawthorne (1804–1864). Hawthorne later described his experiences there in *The Blithedale Romance* (1852). Many other leading writers—including **Ralph Waldo Emerson, Bronson Alcott, Margaret Fuller, Theodore Parker,** and **Orestes Brownson** (*see all*)—visited Brook Farm. Its most outstanding feature was its school, which attempted to establish "perfect freedom of intercourse between students and teaching body." In 1846, a fire destroyed a newly built central building, and Brook Farm was forced to close the following year.

BROWNSON, Orestes (1803–1876). Brownson was a writer of the New England school of **Transcendentalism** (*see*) and at various times during his life was a member of five different religions. During his career, he was concerned with the conditions under which most laborers worked, and in 1828 he founded the short-lived Workingmen's Party. A native of Vermont, he first joined the Presbyterian Church when he was 19 but left it to become a Universalist minister in 1826. Six years later, he converted to the more liberal Unitarianism. In 1836, Brownson formed his own church—the Society for Christian Union and Progress. Two years later, he established the *Boston Quarterly Review,* in which he attacked organized Christianity, inherited wealth, and prison conditions. The journal was renamed *Brownson's Quarterly Review* in 1844. Brownson was a member of the Transcendental Club and was closely associated with **Henry David Thoreau** (*see*). His conversion to Catholicism in 1844 shocked most New England liberals. To explain why he had changed religions so often, he wrote *The Convert; or, Leaves from My Experience,* which was published in 1857.

BRYANT, William Cullen (1794–1878). A noted poet and editor, Bryant raised American verse to new heights of technical achievement and elevated journalism to a respected and influential profession. Born and reared on farmlands in western Massachusetts, Bryant was inspired to write poetry by the natural beauty of his surroundings. He received little formal schooling and halfheartedly prepared for a legal career. Meanwhile, he composed what is

MRS. ROBERT BLOKE WATSON

Brook Farm was forced to close after the main building (left) burned in 1846.

considered one of his finest poems, "Thanatopsis," in 1811. It dwelt lyrically on the question of man's mortality, and when published in 1817, made him famous. Bryant became a lawyer in 1815 and practiced until 1824, when he decided to devote himself entirely to writing. Within one 18-month period, he composed more than 20 poems, among them "Rizpah," "Monument Mountain," "Autumn Woods," and "Forest Hymn." In all, he was to write about 160 poems. By 1825, Bryant was considered the nation's leading poet. From 1829 to 1878, Bryant served as editor and part owner of the New York *Evening Post*. His high writing standards, eloquence, moral dedication, and sound judgment soon made the newspaper a model for other journals to emulate. Editorially, Bryant defended Andrew Jackson (1767–1845), free trade, and the rights of the workingman. He denounced any form of slavery and coined the phrase, "Truth crushed to earth, shall rise again." Although a Democrat for many years, Bryant came out in support of the newly formed antislavery Republican Party in 1856. After the Civil War, he advocated a policy of moderation toward the defeated South and was involved in various charitable and civic movements.

C

CALIFORNIA ARGONAUTS. The California Argonauts—or forty-niners as they were also called—was the name given to the thousands of prospectors who raced to the West Coast during the **gold rush** (*see*) once the news broke that the precious metal had been discovered there in 1848.

From the Atlantic seaboard and Europe, they sped to the gold-fields. Some came by ship (*see pp. 472–473*), but most traveled overland, following the **Oregon Trail** (*see*). The Argonauts were named after the legendary Greek seamen who sailed aboard the *Argo* with Jason in search of the Golden Fleece. Those who came from France were also known as Keskydees, because they often asked, *"Qu'est-ce qu'il dit?"* meaning, "What is he saying?"

CARSON, Christopher ("Kit") (1809–1868). Scout, trapper, hunter, and Indian agent, Kit Carson ranks with **Daniel Boone** (*see*) and Davy Crockett (1786–1836) as one of the most famous frontiersmen in American history. Born in Kentucky, Carson spent his youth in the Boones' Lick district of Missouri, a region then still harassed by Indians. After his mother apprenticed him to a saddler, Carson, then 17, joined a hunting party bound for present-day New Mexico. Making Taos his home base, he spent the next 14 years hunting and trapping throughout the West and Southwest and married an Arapaho girl, who died in 1842. From that year until 1846, he was a guide on all three major expeditions of **John C. Fremont** (*see*) into California and the Northwest. Carson was awarded the rank of lieutenant for his service, and when the Mexican War broke out, he saved the besieged American forces at San Pasqual, California, in 1846 by crawling through the enemy lines to summon a relief force from nearby San Diego. Carson was made a brigadier general in the Union Army during the Civil War and conducted campaigns against the Apaches, Comanches, Kiowas,

Kit Carson

LIBRARY OF CONGRESS: BRADY-HANDY COLLECTION

and Navahos in the Southwest. He served twice (1853–1860 and 1865–1868) as the United States Indian agent at Taos. Unable to read or write until he was over 50, Carson dictated his memoirs to an army officer about 1857. Upon hearing parts of the finished biography read back to him, Carson said that the writer had "laid it on a leetle too thick." In 1868, Carson moved to Colorado, where he died that same year. Carson City, the capital of Nevada, is named in his honor.

CATLIN, George (1796–1872). Catlin's paintings of American Indians provide an accurate source of information about the tribes of the West (*see pp. 498–499 and bottom pp. 501 and 506*). As a boy in Pennsylvania, Catlin learned Indian lore from his mother, who was once an Indian captive, and from the trappers, explorers, and Indian fighters who stopped at his home. He taught himself to paint while studying to be a lawyer. He then briefly practiced law, but in 1823 decided to make his living as a portrait artist. Catlin was inspired to his life's work when he saw a delegation of Western In-

NEW-YORK HISTORICAL SOCIETY

Catlin (right) hid under a wolfskin to sketch a Sioux buffalo hunt in 1832.

dians in all their tribal regalia in Philadelphia. Between 1829 and 1838, he traveled across thousands of miles of wilderness, acquainting himself with 48 known tribes, including the Sioux and the Comanches, faithfully recording their natural surroundings, dress, and customs. Often Catlin's pictorial observations were supplemented by written commentary. "A Comanche on his feet," he noted, "is out of his element . . . but the moment he lays his hand upon his horse . . . he gracefully flies away like a different being." In all, Catlin executed more than 470 full-length Indian portraits and 700 sketches and also wrote several accounts of life among the Indians.

CHAPMAN, John (1775?–1847). Chapman, who was popularly known as Johnny Appleseed, spent most of his life in the wilderness of the Ohio River Valley, planting apple seeds, tending

them, and then giving the young plants to settlers. Born in Massachusetts, Johnny first appeared in the Ohio area in 1801 with a horse load of seeds that he planted around Licking Creek. From 1806 on, he became a familiar figure in the area, always seeking fertile land to plant seeds where future settlements would be likely to grow. A small, wiry man with "eyes that sparkled with a peculiar brightness," he dressed in cast-off clothing or a coffee sack and often went barefoot. He especially loved children and living creatures—even, some say, mosquitoes—and made friends with the Indians he encountered. Wherever he traveled, he also left religious books, and he liked to read to settlers from the New Testament "news right fresh from heaven." About 1838, Johnny headed west into present-day Indiana to continue his good deeds. After his death nine years later in a settler's cabin, many leg-

ends spread about what he had achieved—and Johnny Appleseed became a national folk hero.

CHEVES, Langdon (1776–1857). Cheves was responsible for rescuing the Second Bank of the United States from mismanagement and was called in his day the Hercules of the United States Bank. Born of Scottish parents in South Carolina, Cheves was admitted to the bar at the age of 21 and became one of the most successful lawyers in Charleston. His interest in politics led him from city and state offices into the House of Representatives (1811–1815), where he joined the "war-hawk" group that precipitated the War of 1812 with Britain. Succeeding Henry Clay (1777–1852) as House Speaker in 1814, Cheves at first was against the establishment of a national bank. However, when the Second Bank was opened in 1817, only to run out of funds within two years, Cheves agreed to serve as its president. Before resigning in 1822, he had successfully restored the bank's credit. Cheves returned to South Carolina in 1829 and soon found himself in public opposition to that state's attempt to nullify certain federal tariff laws. Over the next two decades, Cheves gradually abandoned his pro-Union beliefs. By 1850, he had become a strong advocate of a Southern confederacy, although he still opposed secession.

CLARK, William. *See* **Lewis and Clark expedition.**

CLAYTON–BULWER TREATY. This treaty, one of the most controversial in American history, provided that the United States and Britain would share control of any canal built across the Isthmus of Panama. The agreement, which was signed on April 15, 1850, was named for its two negotiators—American Secretary of State John Middleton Clayton (1796–1856) and the British minister to the United States, Sir Henry Bulwer (1801–1872). The idea of linking the Atlantic and Pacific Oceans became popular once gold was discovered in California in 1848. However, Britain occupied parts of Central America and also realized the practicality of a route that would make trading and travel between ports on the two oceans easier. The dispute that ensued over who had rights to construct a connection was settled with the signing of the Clayton-Bulwer Treaty. Both nations pledged neutrality in Central America and promised not to fortify any canal that was built. However, American advocates of expansionism were especially incensed that the accord granted Britain equal rights in the area, saying it ran counter to the Monroe Doctrine. No attempt to build a canal was made in the 19th century, and the treaty was finally superseded by the Hay-Pauncefote Treaty of 1901. This treaty granted America exclusive rights to build a canal that would be open to vessels of all nations. Three years later, construction began on the Panama Canal. The first vessels passed through it in 1914.

CLYMAN, James (1792–1881). Clyman's diaries, compiled during his 37 years as a guide, trapper, and Indian fighter, provide a valuable account of life on the American frontier. Born in Virginia, Clyman moved with his family to Pennsylvania about 1806 and from there to present-day Ohio. After service against hostile Indians in the War of 1812, Clyman began a life of wandering and adventure that took him over much of the western part of the continent. Together with **Jedediah Smith** and **Thomas Fitzpatrick** (*see both*), Clyman was among the first to travel through the South Pass of the Rockies into California. Clyman got lost on the return trip and walked alone through 600 miles of wilderness back to Missouri. During the Black Hawk War of 1832, he served in the same company with Abraham Lincoln (1809–1865). In 1850, he settled on a ranch in Napa, California. His diaries were first published as a book in 1928.

COOPER, James Fenimore (1789-1851). Cooper, who was the first great American novelist, was a prolific writer whose most famous works are the *Leatherstocking Tales*. These five novels—*The Pioneers* (1823), *The Last of the Mohicans* (1826), *The Prairie* (1827), *The Pathfinder* (1840), and *The Deerslayer* (1841)—are named for their hero, a frontiersman called Natty Bumppo, or Leatherstocking. They depict the clash between the wilderness and civilization in American frontier life and contain an idealized portrait of the American Indian that still remains vivid in the American imagination. Cooper grew up on his family's estate at Cooperstown, New York. He entered Yale College at 13 but was expelled for some minor disciplinary reason three years later. He then went to sea and in 1808 joined the United States Navy as a midshipman, serving for three years. Afterward, Cooper married and settled down to the life of a country gentleman in New York State. He was reading a novel to his wife one day and told her that he could write a better one himself. Although his first work, *Precau-* *tion* (1820), was a failure, his second novel, *The Spy* (1821)—a patriotic romance set in New England at the time of the Revolution—gained widespread acclaim. It established his reputation and introduced the formula of flight and pursuit characteristic of most of his subsequent novels. While he was traveling in Europe between 1826 and 1833, Cooper's literary output included several books dealing with the American scene and life aboard American ships. After he returned home, Cooper developed a critical attitude toward American life. In *A Letter to His Countrymen* (1834) and *The American Democrat* (1838), he attacked the absence of true democracy and patriotism in America, and as a result, was frequently criticized for his views. Cooper also wrote a scholarly *History of the Navy of the United States* (1839), as well as many fictional and historical romances about naval life and New York society. His last novel, *The Ways of the Hour* (1850), is an early version of the modern mystery story.

D

DISTRIBUTION–PREEMPTION ACT OF 1841. This law, like the **Preemption Act of 1830** (*see*), legalized preemption—that is, the right of squatters to settle on land before it was sold by the federal government and later to purchase their land directly from the government for $1.25 an acre. In addition, the Distribution-Preemption Act provided that the money received by the federal government from the land sales would be distributed to all the states of the Union through a formula based on population. This feature was suspended in 1842.

DIX, Dorothea Lynde (1802–1887). For almost 50 years, Miss Dix crusaded to have the insane treated as victims of mental illness rather than as criminals or beings possessed by devils. A native of Maine, she taught school at the age of 14 and from 1821 to 1834 ran a school for girls in Boston. During this period, she wrote many stories and books for children. In 1841, while conducting a religious class in the East Cambridge, Massachusetts, jail, Miss Dix saw that the insane were treated brutally. This led to a two-year investigation of institutions where the insane were confined. She found the mentally ill kept "in *cages, closets, cellars, stalls, pens! Chained, naked, beaten with rods,* and *lashed* into obedience!" Despite the apathy she often encountered, Miss Dix devoted the rest of her life to correcting these conditions. Within one three-year period, she estimated that she had visited 18 Massachusetts penitentiaries, 300 county jails and houses of correction, and more than 500 hospitals and houses of charity. Miss Dix was responsible for the building or enlargement of hospitals for the insane in 15 states as well as many institutions in Canada and in Europe. Her humanitarian efforts on behalf of the mentally ill were interrupted during the Civil War, when she served the Union as superintendent of women nurses.

DUNBAR, William (1749–1810). The son of a Scottish lord, Dunbar immigrated to America in 1771 and became known as one of the nation's foremost scientists. His interest in chemistry and mechanics led to his appointment in 1804 by President Thomas Jefferson (1743–1826) to explore the Ouachita River region in present-day Louisiana and Arkansas. This was followed by a similar exploration of the Red River in 1805. Dunbar studied the sign language used by the Indians of the Louisiana Territory and reported on the animal and plant life of the area. He also constructed his own observatory in Mississippi to watch lunary rainbows, which occur occasionally at night after a summer storm when the moon is full, and other meteorological phenomena.

E

EASTMAN, Seth (1808–1875). A professional soldier and expert draftsman, Eastman became interested in Indian life while serving at army outposts in the Midwest and Texas, and he painted a number of scenes depicting the American frontier (*see p. 466*). Born in what is now Maine, Eastman graduated from West Point in 1829 and was first assigned to service in Wisconsin and Minnesota. He was put on the retired list during the Civil War, and after it was over, did nine paintings of Indian life and 17 views of army forts for the Capitol in Washington, D.C.

EDDY, Thomas (1758–1827). A social reformer, Eddy was instrumental in establishing decent prisons and revising the penal code in New York City. Eddy was born in Philadelphia. He settled in New York City sometime about 1790 and became a wealthy insurance broker. Eddy spent more than 25 years of his life fighting for prison reforms, such as jails with individual cells, especially for hardened criminals. He also helped to establish a free school for poor children in 1805 that was a forerunner of the city's public school system.

EMBREE, Elihu (1782–1820). Embree published what is believed to be the first newspaper devoted entirely to the abolition of slavery —the *Manumission Intelligencer,* a weekly that he started in March, 1819. The paper was later issued monthly as the *Emancipator.* Born in Pennsylvania, Embree moved to present-day Tennessee about 1790 and became an iron manufacturer with his brother. About 1815, he joined the Quakers, freed his slaves, and became a member of the newly formed Manumission Society of Tennessee. Embree believed that "freedom is the inalienable right of *all men.*"

EMERSON, Ralph Waldo (1803–1882). Known as the Sage of Concord, Emerson was the spiritual and intellectual leader of New England **Transcendentalism** (*see*) and one of America's early great philosophers. Born and raised in Boston, the son of a Unitarian minister, Emerson was educated for the clergy at Harvard College. After his graduation in 1821, he taught for a while in a local private school for young ladies. He soon returned to the Harvard Divinity School and was licensed to preach in 1826. His career in the pulpit, however, was brief. The death of his first wife in 1831, after only two years of marriage, plunged the young cleric into despair. He toured Europe, and after his return, continued to preach for a few years, but a second career as a writer and lecturer soon consumed all his time. Emerson was deeply influenced by the Transcendentalist philosophers of Europe—men such as Immanuel Kant (1724–1804)—who believed that true knowledge transcended human experience and observation and could only be sensed intuitively. This system of thought appealed to Emerson partly because of his growing concern with materialism in American society. *"Things are in the saddle,/And ride mankind,"* he wrote in "Ode Inscribed to W. H. Channing." As his fame spread, Emerson attracted many of the brightest and most talented writers to his new home in Concord, Massachusetts. He became the leader of an informal group called the Transcendentalist Club, whose membership included **Henry David Thoreau, Margaret Fuller, Theodore Parker** (*see all*), and the Reverend George Ripley (1802–1880). Between 1840 and 1844, they published an influential literary magazine, *The Dial,* in which they probed the nature of transcendental truth in essays and poems. The ideas set forth by Emerson proved highly attractive on the lecture circuit, carrying him as far west as Illinois and providing him with enough income to spend half of each year at his writing desk. The only place where Emerson was not welcome as a speaker was in the South, where his antislavery views (*see* **abolitionists**) were resented. In a series of famous essays—including "Nature" (1836), "Self-Reliance" (1841), and "The American Scholar" (1837)—he developed his main ideas for a truly American approach to life and literature. Many of these ideas were ridiculed by the established intellectual community of his day. In one instance, the professors at his alma mater, Harvard, were so incensed at the Phi Beta Kappa speech he gave there in 1837 that they did not invite him back for 30 years. By the turn of the century, however, Emerson's philosophy was being taught at Harvard

NEW YORK PUBLIC LIBRARY

Ralph Waldo Emerson

in a classroom building named for him. Today he is also celebrated as a poet, whose most popular poem, "Concord Hymn," says of the Revolutionary War battle at Concord's Old North Bridge:

By the rude bridge that arched the flood,
Their flag to April's breeze unfurled,
Here once the embattled farmers stood,
And fired the shot heard round the world.

F

FINNEY, Charles G. (1792–1875). Finney was a revivalist and educator whose converts provided much of the leadership in the reform movements that swept the nation prior to the Civil War. A native of western New York, Finney became a lawyer and did not own a Bible until he came across references to Mosaic law in his practice. While studying it, he said he seemed to see God standing before him. Overwhelmed with

joy, Finney set about converting others. From 1825 to 1837, he conducted revivals, chiefly in the Northeast and Midwest, at which he urged true Christians to join reform movements. One of Finney's chief converts was **Theodore Weld** (*see*). Supported by wealthy New York merchants, Finney established a theological department at Oberlin College in Ohio in 1835. He also served as president of Oberlin (1851–1866) and was prominent in the abolition and temperance movements as well as the campaign for woman suffrage.

FITZPATRICK, Thomas ("Tom") (1799?–1854). Together with **Kit Carson** and **Jim Bridger** (*see both*), Fitzpatrick was one of the great mountain men, as the fur trappers of the Rocky Mountain area were popularly called. Fitzpatrick was born in Ireland and came to America before he was 17. He headed west to seek his fortune and first became a trapper in an expedition up the Missouri River in 1823. The next year he was second in command of the party led by **Jedediah Smith** (*see*) that discovered South Pass in the Wyoming wilderness. Fitzpatrick continued to lead trapping parties until the decline of the fur trade in the late 1830s, when he became a guide. He led the first overland migrations bound for California (1841) and Oregon (1842). He then guided **John C. Fremont** (*see*) on his second expedition (1843–1844) to what are now Oregon, Nevada, and California and also was chief guide for Stephen W. Kearny (1794–1848) in his expeditions to South Pass (1845) and Santa Fe (1846). From 1846 until his death, Fitzpatrick was a government Indian agent for the tribes living near the upper Platte and Arkansas Rivers. Trusted and respected by Arapahos, Cheyennes, and Sioux, he negotiated peace treaties with several tribes and made the arrangements for the first **Treaty of Fort Laramie** (*see*) in 1851.

FORREST, Edwin (1806–1872). Forrest was the first American-born actor to win national acclaim. Before he appeared on the stage, the most successful actors in American theaters came from abroad. Born in Philadelphia, Forrest showed a talent for the stage as a youth by impersonating his family's minister. He made his debut at 14 and went on to play in theaters in Pittsburgh, Cincinnati, and other towns along the Ohio River, as well as in New Orleans. In 1825, Forrest went to Albany, New York, where he acted with the famous English Shakespearean actor Edmund Kean (1787–1833). The following year, Forrest himself became a national idol when he portrayed Othello in New York. He soon became one of America's highest-paid actors and encouraged native talent by offering cash prizes for plays by American writers. His long-standing professional rivalry

LIBRARY OF CONGRESS: MATHEW BRADY COLLECTION

Edwin Forrest

with William Charles Macready (1793–1873), a popular English tragedian, resulted in the terrible Astor Place Riot in New York on May 10, 1849. Forrest's fans mobbed and stoned the Astor Place Opera House, where Macready was performing, and the militia was summoned. In the ensuing fight, the English actor escaped, but 22 persons were killed and 36 were injured. Forrest, whose personal reputation was seriously damaged by the riot, was later involved in a much-publicized divorce case against his wife in 1851. Forrest lost the case and five appeals over the next 18 years, but he continued to appear on the stage to packed theaters until his death.

FORTY-NINERS. *See* **California Argonauts.**

FOSTER, Stephen Collins (1826–1864). Although untrained as a musician, Foster wrote many of the nation's favorite songs and was the most famous American composer of his day. The son of a Pittsburgh merchant, Foster showed an early talent for music and no interest whatsoever in schooling. Instead of going to college, he was tutored at home and in 1846 went to work as a bookkeeper for his brother in Cincinnati. While there, he wrote *O Susanna* in 1848. The song quickly became the anthem of the **California Argonauts** (*see*) and was sung throughout the world. About this time, the most popular entertainment in theaters across the nation was the minstrel show —a series of comedy and dramatic acts interspersed with tunes sung by white "minstrels" whose faces were blackened with burnt cork. From the beginning, the most popular numbers in these

variety shows were Foster's songs. Whether fast and comic or mournful and sentimental, they expressed perfectly the spirit of mid-19th-century America. Foster followed *O Susanna* with, among others, *Camptown Races* (1850), *My Old Kentucky Home* (1853), *Jeanie with the Light Brown Hair* (1854), and *Old Black Joe* (1860). Foster moved to New York City in 1860 to be closer to his publishers. He continued to write songs, but most of them were mediocre in comparison with his earlier ones. Although he earned a lot of money, Foster spent it as quickly as he made it, and he died penniless.

FREEMAN, Thomas (?–1821). Freeman emigrated from Ireland to the United States in 1784 and became an explorer of America's Southwest. He was a surveyor of Washington, D.C., from 1794 to 1796. Following the Louisiana Purchase in 1803, President Thomas Jefferson (1743–1826) decided to send out expeditions to explore the still uncharted western boundaries of the vast Louisiana Territory. He chose Freeman for one of the expeditions. Freeman and a party of 20 men set out in 1806 in two flatboats from Fort Adams in present-day Mississippi to explore the Red and Arkansas Rivers. The expedition took three months to reach a point near where the present boundaries of Oklahoma, Arkansas, and Texas meet. At this point, the Spaniards, who still claimed control of the area, forced the group to turn back. However, as a result of the data collected by Freeman, the course of the lower Red River was accurately charted. The following year, he mapped the Tennessee-Alabama boundary and in 1811 was appointed surveyor of the

United States' public lands south of Tennessee, a post he held until his death.

FREMONT, John C. (1813–1890). One of the most colorful Americans of the 19th century, Fremont was an army officer who established a reputation as an accomplished explorer and became the first Republican Party candidate for the Presidency in 1856. In 1838, as a lieutenant in the army, he accompanied the French explorer J. N. Nicollet (1786–1843) on an expedition to the plateau area between the Mississippi and Missouri Rivers, learning much from the scientifically experienced Nicollet. In 1840, Fremont met Jesse Benton (1824–1902), daughter of Senator Thomas Hart Benton (1782–1858) of Missouri. Benton tried to break up the romance that developed, but the couple married secretly in 1841. Confronted by the fact, Benton relented and became a major backer of Fremont's plans for exploration. A year after his marriage, Fremont set out on his first important expedition. With **Kit Carson** (*see*) as a guide, Fremont mapped much of the **Oregon Trail** (*see*) and scaled a peak in the Rockies that is known today as Fremont Peak. His report, which included data about the terrain and climate, encouraged the settlement of the West. In 1843, Fremont left on a second expedition to map the rest of the Oregon Trail. He crossed the Sierra Nevada into present-day California. This was followed two years later by a third expedition, again to California. While there, Fremont commanded troops in the war against Mexico, and after the American victory, was appointed governor by **Robert F. Stockton** (*see*), naval commander

COURTESY CHICAGO HISTORICAL SOCIETY

John C. Fremont

of American forces in the Pacific. In the squabble that then broke out between Stockton and General Stephen W. Kearny (1794–1848) over who had authority in California, Fremont decided to back Stockton. As a result, the army court-martialed him for mutiny and disobedience. Although President **James K. Polk** (*see*) canceled his punishment, Fremont resigned from the army. He later settled in California and became one of the first two Senators from the territory (1850–1851). Although born and raised in the South, Fremont was opposed to slavery, and in 1856 the newly formed Republican Party chose him as its candidate for President. He lost by a narrow margin to James Buchanan (1791–1868). At the beginning of the Civil War, Fremont was appointed commander of the Department of the West, with headquarters in St. Louis. Missouri was a slave state, and as the Union commander, Fremont was in a difficult position. He declared martial law and ordered that all slaves owned by rebels be freed. At the same time, he confiscated the property of all slave owners. President Abraham

Lincoln (1809–1865) disapproved of the emancipation and removed Fremont from command. Nominated by the Radical Republicans for President in 1864, Fremont withdrew from the campaign when Lincoln agreed to remove Montgomery Blair (1813–1883), a conservative serving as Postmaster General, from the cabinet. After the war, Fremont squandered his fortune on railroad schemes that failed. He later served as governor of the Arizona Territory (1878–1883).

FULLER, Margaret (1810–1850). An author and crusader for women's rights, Miss Fuller was a member of the literary and intellectual movement known as **Transcendentalism** (*see*). She counted among her friends **Ralph Waldo Emerson, Henry David Thoreau** (*see both*), and Nathaniel Hawthorne (1804–1864). From 1839 to 1844, Miss Fuller supported herself by conducting conversation classes on literary and social topics for young women in Boston. Her first book, *Woman in the Nineteenth Century* (1845), was based on these discussions. While still in Boston, Miss Fuller edited *The Dial,* a literary journal, with Emerson and George Ripley (1802–1880). Invited to New York in 1844 by Horace Greeley (1811–1872), she became literary editor of the *New York Tribune* and was soon recognized as one of the most astute critics in America. She left the *Tribune* two years later to move to Rome, where she married Marquis Angelo Ossoli (1820?–1850). Together with her husband, she took part in the movement for the unification of Italy in the late 1840s. Returning to America in 1850, she and her family were drowned in a shipwreck off Fire Island, New York.

G

GARRISON, William Lloyd (1805–1879). One of the foremost **abolitionists** (*see*) of his day, Garrison sought the "immediate and complete emancipation" of slaves. The Massachusetts-born reformer, a printer by trade, made his first antislavery speech at a Boston church in 1829 and for the next 35 years devoted himself entirely to the abolitionist cause. He edited various newspapers and founded his own periodical, the *Liberator*, in 1831. Garrison set forth his credo in the first issue, "I am in earnest—I will not retreat a single inch—and *I will be heard.*" The magazine contained antislavery propaganda written in such inflammatory words that it soon gained world renown, despite its small circulation. In his publication, Garrison denounced the use of force or political activity to free the slaves. Instead, he relied on moral persuasion to convince Americans that slavery was evil. He had no practical plan for abolishing slavery, nor did he ever consider the social problems that would be created by the sudden emancipation of the slaves. Heaping bitter invective on slave owners and moderate abolitionists alike, Garrison's uncompromising extremism soon led to dissension within abolitionist ranks. In 1833, Garrison helped to found the American Anti-Slavery Society, an organization of radical abolitionists. Moderate abolitionists engaged in politics and eventually formed the Republican Party. In the 1840s, Garrison began advocating the secession of the North from the Union, because the federal government tolerated slavery. At an abolitionist gathering on the Fourth of July, 1854, he tossed

LIBRARY OF CONGRESS: BRADY–HANDY COLLECTION

William Lloyd Garrison

a copy of the Constitution into a fire, saying, "So perish all compromises with tyranny." Garrison welcomed the secession of the South in 1861 because the Union would thus have fewer slave states, and initially, he opposed the Civil War. When Abraham Lincoln (1809–1865) issued the Emancipation Proclamation in 1862, Garrison supported it, and the feuding factions of the abolitionist movement were reunited. With the Union victory in 1865, Garrison ceased publishing the *Liberator* and turned his attention to promoting the temperance movement, equal rights for women, and justice for Indians.

GOLD RUSH. The gold rush was a frenzied migration of fortune seekers from all over the world to California (*see pp. 469–485*). It was triggered by the discovery of gold on January 24, 1848, on the estate of **John Sutter** (*see*) near present-day Sacramento. Word quickly spread, and prospectors and merchants—as well as gamblers and gunmen—dashed madly to the Sierra Nevada in search of

wealth. Few found it. Although more than \$200,000,000 in gold had been discovered by 1852, only a few made fortunes, and most **California Argonauts** (*see*) left empty-handed. The majority of the gold found was pure gold, occurring in small quantities in gravel or sand in mountain streams. Prospectors generally used a pan or basin in which gold flakes, which are heavier than sand, were allowed to settle. More efficient mechanical devices were occasionally employed. The most important effect of the gold rush was the large immigration of settlers to California. San Francisco, a village of about 800 in early 1848, found itself with more than 20,000 inhabitants in a matter of months. "Boom towns" such as Placerville, near Sacramento, sprang up overnight. The population of California increased from 15,000 in 1848 to 100,000 the following year and to 250,000 by 1852. Sutter, a wealthy man when gold was first discovered on his property, died

KNOEDLER GALLERIES

A well-equipped prospector rides off to dig for gold in the hills of California.

bankrupt after bonanza hunters devastated his land.

GREAT MEDICINE ROAD. *See* **Oregon Trail.**

H

HALE, Sarah (1788–1879). One of the first women in the field of publishing, Mrs. Hale was for 40 years literary editor (1837–1877) of *Godey's Lady's Book,* the most popular women's magazine at that time in America. Her early writing caught the attention of the Reverend John L. Blake (1788–1857), who in 1828 offered her the opportunity to edit a new monthly women's periodical in Boston. Mrs. Hale went on to edit and write essays, poems, and literary criticism for the *Ladies' Magazine* until 1837. When the magazine was purchased that year by *Godey's Lady's Book,* she became literary editor. Mrs. Hale also wrote books of prose and verse, one of which included the well-known poem "Mary Had a Little Lamb." Her most widely read book was *Woman's Record, or Sketches of Distinguished Women,* published in 1853. Throughout her career, Mrs. Hale campaigned for the establishment of liberal arts colleges and medical schools for women. Matthew Vassar (1792–1868), the founder of Vassar College (1861), was influenced by her ideas.

HARDING, Chester (1792–1866). Harding was a self-taught portraitist who painted many prominent Americans, including Daniel Boone, whom he portrayed in 1819 (*see p. 454*). Born in Massachusetts, Harding served briefly as a drummer boy in the War of 1812. After a varied career as a

drum maker, chair maker, tavern keeper, and house and sign painter, he established himself as a portraitist in Paris, Kentucky. He later set up studios also in St. Louis, Washington, D.C., Boston, and Northampton, Massachusetts, enjoying enormous popular success. He finally settled in Springfield, Massachusetts, in 1830.

HARNEY, William S. (1800–1889). A career military officer and Indian fighter, Harney joined the army in 1818 and first served in campaigns against the Seminoles in Florida. During the Mexican War, he became the hero of the Battle of Cerro Gordo on April 17–18, 1847, by leading the charge that led to an American victory. On September 3, 1855, he commanded federal troops in their victory over the Sioux Indians at Sand Hill on the North Platte River. As a result, Harney was given command of the Department of Oregon. However, he alienated the British by occupying San Juan Island, which the British claimed, and was subsequently replaced. At the outbreak of the Civil War, Harney, who had married a St. Louis woman and had many friends who were for slavery, was relieved of his duties as commander of the Department of the West. He retired in 1863 and was later given the rank of major general.

HARPER, Robert Goodloe (1765–1825). A Southerner, Harper was an original member of the **American Colonization Society** (*see*), which was established in 1817 to settle free American blacks in Africa. He hoped that the removal of free blacks from the South would lead to the creation of a white labor force. Harper gave the name Liberia to the Society's Afri-

can colony and also named Monrovia, its present capital, after President James Monroe (1758–1831). Born on a Virginia farm and raised in North Carolina, Harper served in the Revolution under Nathanael Greene (1742–1786). He graduated from the College of New Jersey (now Princeton University) in 1785 and became a lawyer in South Carolina. He served in that state's legislature and later in the House of Representatives (1795–1801). At first a Democratic-Republican, Harper switched his allegiance to the Federalist Party and became a leading opponent of Thomas Jefferson (1743–1826). In 1801, Harper moved his law practice to Baltimore. He was a major general with Maryland troops during the War of 1812. Harper was elected a Senator from Maryland in 1816, but he resigned his seat the same year because his business activities took so much time.

J

JOHNNY APPLESEED. *See* **Chapman, John.**

L

LADD, William (1778–1841). Known as the apostle of peace, Ladd formulated the first detailed plan for a world peace organization. The son of a wealthy New Hampshire captain, Ladd also went to sea after graduating from Harvard in 1797. After 1812, he settled in Maine and became interested in establishing peace throughout the world. In 1828, Ladd founded the **American Peace Society** (*see*), and in order to enlist the aid of churches, became a Congregational minister nine years

COLLECTION OF DR. WILLIAM E. LADD

William Ladd

later. He preached tirelessly, refusing to obey his physician's advice to rest his legs, which were so badly ulcerated that he had to speak sitting down. In 1840, Ladd proposed the establishment of a congress of nations to create international laws and an international court to arbitrate disputes between countries. Embodied in *An Essay on a Congress of Nations,* his ideas provided the basis for subsequent pacifist organizations. The American Peace Society continued its activities until the United Nations was founded in 1945.

LAND ACT OF 1820. Passed by Congress on April 24, 1820, the Land Act of 1820 abolished the practice of buying public land on credit and lowered the price of land from $1.64 an acre to $1.25 an acre. It also reduced the minimum unit of purchase from 160 acres to 80 acres, but the entire purchase price had to be paid at the time of sale. Prior to this law, not only had public land been more expensive, but the federal government had also extended liberal credit privileges to all purchasers. As a result, the pioneer

settlers in the rapidly expanding West often bought more land than they could afford and ended up heavily in debt. Meanwhile, speculators, who had better financial backing than the settlers, bought up large expanses of land intended for settlement and resold them at exorbitant prices. The Land Act of 1820 was supposed to benefit the pioneer, but even with the lower cost of land, few settlers had enough cash to pay for their land in a lump sum. Thus, the speculator still profited in buying and reselling land, and the settlers had to wait for such legislation as the **Preemption Act of 1830** and the **Distribution-Preemption Act of 1841** (*see both*) before they could buy land.

LARKIN, Thomas (1802–1858). Larkin, a merchant in Monterey, California, was appointed a secret agent by President **James K. Polk** (*see*) in October, 1845, to counter the efforts of French and British agents who were trying to gain control of California. Larkin began a propaganda campaign, warning Californians that their lands might be ceded by Spain to France or Britain. His mission ended when the Mexican War broke out the following spring. Larkin had arrived in Monterey from the Carolinas in 1832. He opened a store and began trading with Mexico and the Hawaiian Islands in lumber, flour, and other goods. He had also profited from land speculation in California. In addition to acting as a confidential agent, Larkin was United States consul in California from 1844 to 1848. He returned to business after serving in the state constitutional convention in 1849.

LESUEUR, Charles (1778–1846). Born in France, Lesueur was an

artist and a naturalist who taught drawing at the community school in **New Harmony** (*see*), Indiana. He came to the United States in 1816 and toured the interior of the country, sketching and painting what he observed in the wilderness. Lesueur then served as curator of the Academy of Natural Sciences of Philadelphia (1817–1825). In 1826, he joined the New Harmony community and remained long after its founder, **Robert Owen** (*see*), had left it. Before returning to France about 1837, Lesueur wrote several papers on North American fishes.

LEWIS, Meriwether. *See* **Lewis and Clark expedition.**

LEWIS AND CLARK EXPEDITION. The expedition led by Meriwether Lewis (1774–1809) and William Clark (1770–1838) successfully traveled from St. Louis to the Pacific Ocean and back—a total of almost 7,700 miles—in two years and four months. Its members collected information on the wilderness of North America that was to have a great influence on future westward expansion. President Thomas Jefferson (1743–1826) had long desired to send a scientific expedition to the Northwest, and in January, 1803, Congress agreed to finance the undertaking. When later that year the United States acquired the vast Louisiana Territory from France, the expedition was assigned to chart the newly acquired lands and to find out if there was a commercially practical water route to the Pacific. In addition, Jefferson wanted to gather information about the Indians in the West and to establish a claim to the Oregon Territory. Lewis, who was the President's secretary, was appointed to lead the expedition. He invited Clark, a close friend, to share command. The two men spent the winter of 1803–1804 at St. Louis, recruiting hunters, boatmen, and Indian interpreters. On May 14, 1804, Lewis and Clark, together with 43 men, including Clark's slave York, set out on a 55-foot-long keelboat and two flatboats. Heading upstream on the Missouri River, by the autumn of 1804 the group had progressed as far as the villages of the Arikara and Mandan Indians in what is now North Dakota. At a site near the present city of Bismarck, Lewis and Clark built a stockade and made their winter camp. There in the spring of 1805, a French interpreter, Toussaint Charbonneau and his pregnant Shoshone Indian wife, **Sacagawea** (*see*), joined the explorers. After Sacagawea gave birth to a son, the party followed the Missouri to its source in the foothills of the Rocky Mountains in present-day Montana. Here, Sacagawea contacted her tribe, which supplied

the expedition with horses to carry baggage over the Rockies. They crossed the Continental Divide —where westward-flowing rivers separate from eastward-flowing ones—at Lemhi Pass in present-day Idaho. The expedition then followed the Clearwater River to the Snake River and at last reached the Columbia River, on which it proceeded downstream to the Pacific. The ocean was sighted on November 7, 1805. The men built shelters a few miles from the mouth of the river, near the present site of Astoria, Oregon, and named the camp Fort Clatsop, after some local Indians. They spent a miserable winter there and on March 23, 1806, headed back east. After recrossing the Rockies, the men split into two groups to make more extensive explorations of the country. Lewis navigated the Marias River, a Montana tributary of the Missouri, while Clark journeyed down the Yellowstone. The leaders met near the confluence of the Mis-

souri and Yellowstone Rivers on the border between Montana and North Dakota and arrived back in St. Louis on September 23, 1806. Of the original group, only two men had been lost—one had apparently died of appendicitis and the other had deserted. The extensive notes Lewis and Clark had taken on the terrain, climate, plants, animals, and Indian customs of the West were subsequently edited by Nicholas Biddle (1786–1844) and published in 1814.

LIBERIA. *See* **American Colonization Society.**

LIBERTY PARTY. Growing opposition to slavery in America brought about the organization of the Liberty Party in 1840. Unlike the fiery abolitionist **William Lloyd Garrison** (*see*), members of the Liberty Party believed political action—not moral argument— was the way to correct social injustices. The party's Presidential

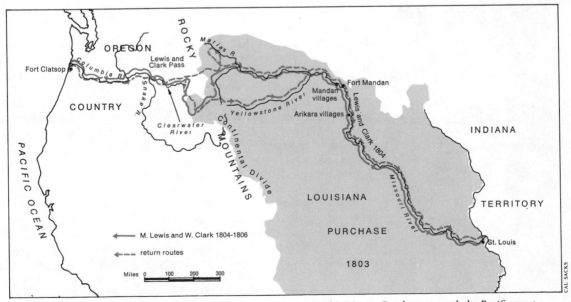

The Lewis and Clark expedition passed through the newly acquired Louisiana Purchase to reach the Pacific coast.

candidate in the election of 1840, **James G. Birney** (*see*), a former slave owner, received only about 7,000 votes. Four years later, however, running on a platform that opposed the annexation of Texas as a slave state, Birney cut deeply into Whig support of Henry Clay (1777–1852) by polling more than 15,000 votes in New York State. This enabled **James K. Polk** (*see*) to receive the state's 36 electoral votes, just enough to win the Presidency. In 1848, members of the Liberty Party joined with antislavery Democrats and Whigs to form the Free-Soil Party.

LIND, Jenny (1820–1887). Known as the Swedish Nightingale, Jenny Lind was one of the most outstanding coloratura sopranos of the 19th century. The range and quality of her voice were reputedly unsurpassed by any other singer. Born in Sweden, Miss Lind began her career in opera in her homeland and appeared also in France, Germany, and England. In 1849, she decided to devote herself en-

LIBRARY OF CONGRESS

Jenny Lind

tirely to concert and oratorio singing. From 1850 to 1852, she toured the United States under the management of the showman **Phineas T. Barnum** (*see*). She was such a phenomenal success that tickets to her concerts were sometimes sold by auction. In 1852, Miss Lind married the German-born composer and conductor Otto Goldschmidt (1829–1907) and toured Europe before finally settling in England.

LONG, Stephen Harriman (1784–1864). An army engineer, Long explored large areas of the American West and played a leading role in the early years of railroad building. Born in New Hampshire, Long entered the engineering corps in 1814 and two years later joined the army's topographical service. In 1817, he explored the upper Mississippi, Fox, and Wisconsin Rivers. In 1819 and 1820, Long commanded an expedition to the Rocky Mountains, where he discovered the peak in northern Colorado that is named for him. The trip was later described by the geologist-explorer Edwin James (1797–1861), who accompanied him. In 1823, Long explored the sources of the St. Peter's (now Minnesota) River and the area along the northern border of the United States west of the Great Lakes. He later became an authority in the field of railroad engineering. He planned routes, served as a consultant to several rail lines, and was an expert in bridge construction. In 1827, Long helped to lay out the route of the Baltimore & Ohio Railroad, and in 1829 he published the *Rail Road Manual,* the first work of its kind in America.

LUNDY, Benjamin (1789–1839). A pioneer in the abolition move-

ment, Lundy organized the Union Humane Society in 1815 and was the editor of numerous antislavery publications. Born in New Jersey, Lundy became interested in slavery while a saddler's apprentice in Wheeling, Virginia, then a center of the slave trade. In 1821, he published *The Genius of Universal Emancipation,* a newspaper he subsequently wrote and edited wherever he traveled in the nation. In 1827, Lundy was assaulted by a Baltimore slave dealer whom he had criticized in *The Genius.* **William Lloyd Garrison** (*see*), whom Lundy recruited, became associate editor of *The Genius* in 1829 in Baltimore and soon got the paper into lawsuits because of his caustic abolitionist views. Lundy went to Haiti, Canada, and present-day Texas in the 1820s and 1830s in search of sites for colonies that could be settled by freed Negroes. In 1838, three years after the newspaper folded, his property was destroyed by an angry mob in Philadelphia.

M

McGUFFEY, William Holmes (1800–1873). McGuffey was one of the most influential American educators of the 19th century. His series of six *Eclectic Readers* —known popularly as McGuffey's Readers—were published between 1836 and 1857 and sold more than 122,000,000 copies. Born in Pennsylvania, McGuffey moved to Ohio with his parents in 1802. As a youth, he could recite from memory long passages from the Bible and other literature. After graduating from Washington (now Washington and Jefferson) College in Pennsylvania in 1826, he began a long career as a college teacher and administrator. He

NEW-YORK HISTORICAL SOCIETY

A Mormon settler poses with his several wives and children outside his ramshackle cabin in what is now Utah.

taught languages at Miami University in Ohio (1826–1836) and was president of both Cincinnati College (1836–1839) and Ohio University (1839–1843). From 1845 until his death, he was professor of moral philosophy at the University of Virginia. McGuffey was a lifelong advocate of public education and worked to establish public-school systems in both Ohio and Virginia. He also maintained a keen interest in the elementary grades, to which his famous *Readers* were directed. Thirty-seven states adopted his books, which stressed moral and cultural as well as literary values.

MANIFEST DESTINY. "Manifest destiny" was a phrase used in the 1840s by many Americans who believed that the nation was intended by God to control the continent from the Atlantic to the Pacific Oceans. The phrase was coined by **John L. O'Sullivan** (*see*), who, in his *Democratic Review* in 1845, said that it was "our manifest destiny to overspread the continent allotted by Providence for the free development of our yearly multiplying millions." "Manifest

destiny" quickly became a political slogan in the Democratic Party, with Whigs and then Republicans soon joining in the crusade for expansion. The theory behind it was first used by O'Sullivan to justify the Mexican War. Twenty years later, it was employed as a reason for the purchase of Alaska, and before the turn of the century, to justify even the acquisition of Hawaii and Spanish territories in the Pacific.

MILLER, Alfred Jacob (1810–1874). A portrait and landscape artist, Miller made more than 100 sketches of Indian life during an expedition into the Rocky Mountains in the late 1830s. Born in Maryland, Miller studied art in Europe and moved to New Orleans in 1837. There, that same year, Captain William Drummond Stewart, a Scottish baronet, asked Miller to join him on a trip through Indian country to the Rockies (*see pp. 518, 526, and 532–533*). Stewart collected Miller's works for his home, Murthley Castle in Scotland, but watercolor reproductions were later published in America.

MORMONS. The Church of Jesus Christ of Latter-Day Saints, a religious sect usually referred to as Mormons, settled the lands that constitute the present state of Utah. In 1830, **Joseph Smith** (*see*) published his *Book of Mormon* and claimed that he was God's appointed prophet on earth. His followers established a religious community in Fayette, New York. However, "Gentiles," or non-Mormons, regarded these people with suspicion and forced them to migrate, first to Ohio, then to Missouri, and later to Illinois. In 1839, the Mormons founded Nauvoo, Illinois, and free of persecution, enjoyed a few years of prosperity. However, when Smith announced in 1843 that God allowed a man to have more than one wife—a practice known as polygamy—hostility developed not only among Gentiles but also within Mormon ranks. Many Mormons left the church. Following a local anti-Mormon uprising in 1844, Smith and his brother Hyrum were shot to death by an angry mob. Finally expelled from Nauvoo in 1846, his remaining followers, led by **Brigham Young**

COURTESY OF DON BLAIR, NEW HARMONY, INDIANA

Robert Owen envisioned a quadrangle design for his utopian New Harmony.

(*see*), headed west to avoid further persecution. The band settled in the desolate valley of the Great Salt Lake in 1847. They survived initial hardships and within 10 years had irrigated the desert in order to grow crops and had founded Salt Lake City. Young, who was appointed governor (1850–1858) of the Utah Territory, legalized polygamy in 1852. This practice, together with Young's hostility to non-Mormons, eventually caused the federal government to send troops in 1858 to remove him from office. The Mormon Church outlawed polygamy in 1890, and six years later Utah became the 45th state. The Mormon Church's membership now totals almost 4,000,000 Americans.

MOTT, Lucretia (1793–1880). A Quaker minister, Mrs. Mott was a leading spokesman for the abolition of slavery, women's voting rights, and the temperance movement. Born in Massachusetts, she attended the Friends' boarding school near Poughkeepsie, New York, where she later taught and met James Mott (1788–1868), a fellow teacher, whom she married in 1811. At the school, Mrs. Mott first encountered discrimination against women—female teachers were paid half as much as male teachers. After settling in Philadelphia, Mrs. Mott became a Quaker minister and in 1827 joined a liberal wing of the sect, called the Hicksites. Because she denounced slavery in her sermons, the conservative, proslavery Quakers tried unsuccessfully to remove her from the ministry. She helped found the American Anti-Slavery Society (see **abolitionists**) in 1833 and seven years later went with her husband to an international antislavery convention in London. Upon arrival, she and another

abolitionist, **Elizabeth Cady Stanton** (*see*), discovered that they would not be recognized as United States delegates because of their sex, so they decided to start a campaign to win equal rights for women. They arranged the first convention of the feminist movement at Seneca Falls, New York, in 1848. During the Civil War, Mrs. Mott used her home as an asylum for runaway slaves.

MURRIETA, Joaquin (1832?–1853). Murrieta was a notorious bandit who roamed California in the days of the **gold rush** (*see*). He came to California, probably from Sonora, Mexico, about 1849. Outraged by the prejudice and abuse he suffered at the hands of American gold miners, Murrieta organized a gang of desperadoes. For more than two years, he terrorized much of California, robbing and killing (*see p. 479*). In 1853, the state legislature ordered his band of marauders hunted down. Mounted rangers surprised the gang on July 25, 1853, shot Murrieta, and killed or captured most of his followers. Murrieta's head was then exhibited in a bottle throughout the state. Despite his brutality, a legend grew up that Murrieta, much like Robin Hood, had helped the poor. However, there is no evidence of this in Murrieta's life.

N

NEW HARMONY. Situated in southwestern Indiana, New Harmony was one of the earliest experiments in communal living in America and served as a model for similar colonies that sprang up throughout the nation in the 19th century. A group of Pennsylvania Germans had originally estab-

lished a religious-communistic society called Harmonie at the site in 1814. After their venture failed, English philanthropist **Robert Owen** (*see*) purchased the land in 1825 and renamed it New Harmony. Here Owen attempted to create a perfect society, based on principles of reason rather than religion and devoted to bettering the human condition through socialism and free education. Of the nearly 1,000 settlers who came to the colony, most were idealists who were unprepared to handle such practical necessities as managing factories or farms. Because of the lack of any authoritative control, internal strife resulted. Owen, admitting that his experiment was unworkable, dissolved New Harmony in 1828. The community, however, had a lasting effect on American education, for it had established the first kindergarten, trade school, and community-supported public school in the United States.

NOYES, John Humphrey (1811–1886). A social reformer, Noyes founded the **Oneida Community** (*see*), which was the most successful American experiment in communal living in the 19th century. A native of Vermont, Noyes first studied law, but in 1831, the year of a religious revival in New England, he decided to become a minister. While at Yale Theological Seminary in 1833, Noyes helped to found the Free Church of New Haven. The following year, he announced to the congregation that the Second Coming of Christ had already taken place, in A.D. 70. He also denounced the traditional Christian belief that man was born sinful. Instead, he advocated the doctrine of perfectionism, which meant that a person could become sinless, or perfect, if he worked at it. Church authorities, believing Noyes to be insane, revoked his preacher's license. To test his theories, Noyes set up a radical social experiment in 1839 at Putney, Vermont, based on early Christian forms of communism. In 1846, the Putney group abandoned monogamy and began a system of "complex marriage," by which all men and women were married to each other, without rivalry, jealousy, or exclusiveness. Justifying this practice, Noyes wrote some years later that the human heart "is capable of loving any number of times and any number of persons; the more it loves the more it can love." He also instituted birth-control measures, so that women would not suffer from unwanted pregnancies. The righteous citizens of Putney, sensing sexual scandal, had Noyes arrested, but he broke bail and fled with his followers to central New York State, where they founded Oneida in 1848. At Oneida, complex marriage was again practiced, and Noyes also established such strict family-planning procedures that only 44 children were born in 20 years. By 1869, the ranks of Oneidans were visibly dwindling, so Noyes adopted a method of scientific breeding that he called "stirpiculture" to repopulate the colony. However, in order to have children, a couple first had to be judged suitable as parents by a committee. Many of the 58 children born during this experiment became successful and distinguished citizens. Noyes governed the colony for 31 years, and when public opposition to the community increased, abolished the practice of complex marriage in 1879. He then fled to Canada to avoid legal action and later died in Ontario.

O

ONEIDA COMMUNITY.
Founded in central New York State by **John Humphrey Noyes** (*see*) in 1848, Oneida was the most radical social experiment in 19th-century America. Believing that man could become perfect if he were freed from selfish activity, Noyes abolished private property at Oneida and ruled that everything would be owned jointly. To eliminate possessiveness, he also instituted the practice of "complex marriage," which meant that every woman at Oneida was the wife of every man, and vice versa. Couples had to obtain permission from the community in order to have children, and infants were raised in communal nurseries. In the 31 years of its existence, Oneida became wealthy from manufacturing iron traps, silver cutlery, silk, and canned goods. However, outsiders condemned complex marriage as immoral, and the colony was pressured into adopting monogamy in 1879. The sharing of all property was also dropped, and Oneida became a private corporation owned by shareholders, who continued its various commercial enterprises.

OREGON TRAIL.
Known as the Oregon Trail, this major route for pioneers going to what is now Oregon was actually a number of routes that converged where rivers and mountains had to be crossed. Known to the Indians as the Great Medicine Road, it stretched nearly 2,000 miles from Independence, Missouri, to the Willamette Valley. The original trail forded several rivers in Missouri and Kansas, traversed the vast sweep of grasslands in the Great Plains, and then followed the North Platte River and crossed the Rocky Mountains at South Pass, 7,500 feet above sea level. From there the trail finally made its way to the south bank of the Columbia River in the Willamette Valley. The dangers encountered on it were as varied as the land it covered —freezing cold weather, drought, the constant threat of raiding Indians and attacks by wild animals, deep rivers and dangerous rapids, marshes, quicksand, and sand storms. The route was marked with the bones of horses and oxen and the shallow graves of pioneers too foolhardy—and after 1848, too greedy for gold—to travel together. The first immigrant train arrived in Oregon in 1842. By 1845, about 3,000 pioneers had completed the six-month-long trip and settled in Willamette Valley. Their presence strengthened America's position in the Oregon boundary dispute with Britain. A later, southerly route, the Overland Trail, ran only from the confluence of the North and South Platte Rivers in present-day Colorado to Fort Bridger, in what is now Wyoming, where it joined the original trail. The Overland Trail was shorter and less dangerous between these two points, but emigrants continued to favor the Oregon Trail. With the advent of railroads in the 1870s, the trail was abandoned. Although the Lincoln Highway and Union Pacific Railroad closely follow the

Overland Trail, only a few sections of the Oregon Trail are still in use. They are followed by U.S. Route 30.

O'SULLIVAN, John Louis (1813–1895). O'Sullivan, a journalist and diplomat, promoted the cause of American expansion in the 1840s and is credited with coining the phrase **manifest destiny** (*see*). The son of an American sea captain and a graduate of Columbia College in New York City, O'Sullivan practiced law until 1837, when he helped found the *United States Magazine and Democratic Review.* The magazine soon became the chief exponent of the expansionism of its time. In 1839, O'Sullivan wrote, "We are the nation of human progress, and who will, what can, set limits to our onward march?" He saw the nation as destined to embrace all of the North American continent and Cuba. In 1845, he wrote that the right to American expansion lay in "our manifest destiny to occupy and to possess the whole of the Continent which Providence has given us." Nine years later, after he had sold his magazine, O'Sullivan was appointed by President Franklin Pierce (1804–1869) to a diplomatic post in Portugal, where he stayed for four years. Afterward, he lived abroad until about 1871, when he returned to New York and retired.

OVERLAND TRAIL. *See* **Oregon Trail.**

OWEN, Robert (1771–1858). This Welsh-born businessman and social reformer organized utopian communities in England and the United States in the early 19th century. Owen, who made his fortune in Scottish cotton mills, first sought to improve the lives of the

workers in his own factory. He eliminated child labor, established sickness and old-age benefits, and provided recreational facilities for his employees. In 1813, Owen published *A New View of Society,* which contended that men of good character were products of the proper physical, moral, and social environments. To demonstrate his theory, Owen began founding "ideal" communities in which competition was to be eliminated and everyone would share property and profits equally. He came to America himself to found **New Harmony** (*see*), Indiana, in 1825. It failed after three years. Owen retired from business in 1829 and spent the rest of his life and his fortune trying to spread his theories. His son, Robert Dale Owen (1808–1877), lived most of his life in America and was instrumental in founding the **Smithsonian Institution** (*see*) in Washington, D.C., in 1846.

P

PARKER, Theodore (1810–1860). A controversial Unitarian Minister, Parker was a leading abolitionist who was not opposed to the South's seceding from the Union. Born in Massachusetts, Parker was a child prodigy with little formal education. Although too poor to enroll in Harvard, he was permitted to take examinations and was later granted an honorary degree. Parker began teaching at the age of 17. He learned 20 languages and acquired nearly 16,000 books for his library. Parker's writings and sermons often brought him into conflict with church authorities. He doubted the authority of the Bible and urged instead that religion be a science based on data about

God's presence in man and nature. A humanitarian, Parker took part in many efforts to aid escaped slaves. Unlike many abolitionists, however, he believed that the South had a right to secede.

PERRY, Matthew Calbraith (1794–1858). Perry, whose distinguished naval career spanned nearly 50 years, is best remembered as the American who opened Japan to trade in 1854, one of the major diplomatic achievements of the 19th century. A native of Rhode Island, Perry entered the navy as a midshipman in 1809. After serving awhile under his brother, Oliver Hazard Perry (1785–1819), he fought briefly in the War of 1812 against Britain. In 1820 and 1821, he helped establish an African colony for American blacks, later called Liberia (*see* **American Colonization Society**). After various naval missions, which included fighting pirates in the West Indies in 1822, Perry was appointed second officer of the New York (now Brooklyn) Navy Yard in 1833. An early advocate of steam-powered warships, he was influential in furthering naval training. In 1837, he was promoted to captain and given command of the *Fulton,* one of the first steam vessels in the United States Navy. Authorized by the **Webster-Ashburton Treaty** (*see*), Perry led the squadron that went to Africa to suppress the slave trade in the early 1840s. During the Mexican War, he helped capture Veracruz in March, 1847. Five years later, President Millard Fillmore (1800–1874) appointed Perry to go to Japan, where all ports but one had been closed to Western traders since the 17th century. Perry was instructed to negotiate a treaty that would open at least one more port to American shipping and grant protection to

A Japanese artist depicted Perry's officers at a formal banquet in 1854.

BOEHRINGER COLLECTION, MARINER'S MUSEUM

shipwrecked American seamen. Perry, who had been made a commodore, set sail in November with a large fleet, which was meant to impress the Japanese. He arrived at Napa, Great Luchu Island (now Naha, Okinawa) the following May and then sailed to Yedo (now Tokyo) Bay. Despite a cool reception, Perry insisted on meeting with the emperor's representatives, and this was arranged in July. Giving them time to consider the American proposals, he sailed for China, returning to Yedo in February, 1854. On March 31, 1854, at Yokohama, the Treaty of Kanagawa was signed. Under it, Japan granted America trading privileges in the ports of Hakodate and Shimoda and promised to protect shipwrecked American seamen. Perry negotiated a similar treaty with the Luchu Islanders before returning to America in January, 1855. He later wrote an account of his mission, entitled *Narrative of the Expedition of an American Squadron to the China Seas and Japan,* which was published by the government in 1856.

PIKE, Zebulon Montgomery (1779–1813). Pike, a professional soldier, was one of the earliest explorers of the Central and Western Plains. His father was an army officer, and Pike himself was commissioned a first lieutenant at the age of 20. In 1805, Pike led 20 men on his first expedition. He set out from St. Louis, Missouri, in search of the source of the Mississippi River. Pike believed he had found the Mississippi, but later explorations proved that he was mistaken. His next assignment was to explore the headwaters of the Arkansas and Red Rivers. Pike proceeded along the Missouri, Osage, and Arkansas Rivers to the site of present-day Pueblo, Colorado. Near Pueblo, he discovered the peak that was later named in his honor. While searching for the source of the Red River, Pike unknowingly wandered into Spanish territory and built a fort. He was arrested by Spanish troops, who took his papers and maps from him. However, Pike remembered enough of what he had seen to publish an account of his expeditions in 1810. During the War of 1812, Pike, a brigadier general, led a successful attack on York, (now Toronto), Canada, in 1813. He was killed in the battle.

PLAINS INDIANS. Some of the best-known Indians in American history lived in the vast, treeless plains that stretch from the Mississippi River to the Rocky Mountains and from Texas to Canada (see pp. 497–510). Most historians believe that the earliest Indians migrated many thousands of years ago from Siberia, crossing over to Alaska on a spit of land that is now under the Bering Strait. These Indians wandered south and eventually spread throughout North America, splitting up and forming distinctly different tribes as time passed. The early Plains Indians were both farmers who raised corn, squash, and beans and hunters who lived off the herds of bison that roamed the region. At first, the Indians hunted on foot, pulling their few possessions on travois—A-shaped frames made from two poles and a crossbar of wood or rawhide. After they captured horses that strayed from 17th-century Spanish settlements in the Southwest, the Indians soon learned to become excellent riders. The horses made it easier to hunt buffalo, and the Indian population of the Plains increased as tribes from the North, South, and West —the Comanches, Kiowas, Sioux, Navahos, and Apaches—joined the Arikara, Hidatsa, and Mandan Indians who had always lived there. The Indians ate the meat of the buffalo, used its hides for teepees, moccasins, and clothing, and made farming tools, bow strings, and eating utensils from the animal's bones and sinews. Because of the horse's importance in hunting, an Indian's wealth came to be measured by how many horses he had, and wars were fought with other tribes and with the white man in order to obtain more of them. A brave never entered battle without the hope of attaining per-

MUSEUM OF THE AMERICAN INDIAN, HEYE FOUNDATION

Warriors tortured themselves with ropes tied to their skins in the Sun Dance, which is still performed today.

sonal glory, and most young men were members of military societies. In addition to warring, the tribes enjoyed dancing, creating bead and feather art work, and decorating hides. One dance celebrated by nearly all the Plains Indians was the Sun Dance. A mass tribal ceremony, the Sun Dance was usually held in spring, when the Indians regrouped after a long winter of living in sheltered valleys. Visions and dreams believed to be sent by invisible spirits played a large part in the lives of the Plains Indians. A warrior never went into battle unless his dreams were favorable. He painted special signs of power—flashes of lightning, round suns or moons—on his body, his horse, his war shield, and his teepee to give him strength. The language spoken by the Plains Indians consisted of varieties of six distinct languages. Different tribes communicated with one another by means of picture writing, hand signs, and smoke signals. The Indians' way of life was threatened from the 1840s on as the white man moved westward in search of furs, new land, and gold. The whites killed off vast numbers of much-needed buffalo and took

the best grazing lands to build farms or raise cattle. Contact with the whites also lead to epidemics because the Indian had no immunity to diseases such as smallpox, cholera, and measles. In addition, many Indians could not stomach liquor, which whites often bartered in return for pelts and hides. After the white man reached California and large numbers of settlers began farming the Plains, the Indians found themselves fighting a losing battle to retain their old ways.

POINSETT, Joel (1779–1851). Poinsett was Secretary of War (1837–1841) at the time the Seminole Indians of Florida were subdued. The son of a prominent South Carolina physician, Poinsett was educated in England and traveled throughout Europe and to Western Asia. In 1809, he was appointed a United States commissioner in charge of investigating South American political affairs. Upon his return to South Carolina in 1815, Poinsett was elected to the state legislature and then served (1821–1825) in the House of Representatives. In 1825, he accepted an appointment as the first American minister to Mexico. The next four years there were unhappy ones for Poinsett. He was accused of intrigues, opposed by the British envoy, and involved in the unstable politics of the new republic. At Mexico's repeated request, he was recalled in 1829. He brought back a flower that was later named for him—the poinsettia. Poinsett returned to his home state and assumed the leadership of the Union Party there. The party was opposed to secession during South Carolina's political squabbles with President Andrew Jackson (1767–1845) over high tariffs. In 1837, Poinsett

was appointed Secretary of War by President Martin Van Buren (1782–1862) and was responsible for broadening the study program at West Point, directing the military expeditions against the Seminoles and moving nearly 40,000 Indians west across the Mississippi. He retired in 1841.

POLK, James Knox (1795–1849). The nation's 11th President, Polk was determined to extend American control over the Far West and was responsible for getting the United States involved in the war with Mexico in 1845. Although all his goals for expansion were realized, Polk made so many enemies that he did not even try to run for a second term. Born in North Carolina and raised in Tennessee, Polk was a successful lawyer when elected to the first of seven terms (1825–1839) in the House of Representatives. As Speaker of the House (1835–1839), Polk was a firm supporter of the policies of President Andrew Jackson (1767–1845). Polk was elected governor of Tennessee in 1839, but he failed to win a second term in either 1841 or 1843. The following year, Polk became the first dark-horse Presidential candidate when he received the Democratic nomination on the party's ninth convention ballot. He was known to favor the annexation of Texas, while his opponent in the Presidential campaign that followed, Henry Clay (1777–1852), hedged on the issue. Polk's campaign focused on the Texas question. He indicated he would go to war against Britain to get the Oregon boundary line fixed at latitude 54°40'. Polk was elected in a very close race, with the electoral votes of New York deciding the issue. Just prior to Polk's inauguration, President **John Tyler** (*see*), as a final act, signed a bill annexing Texas. As President himself, Polk had four major objectives: (1) the settlement of the Oregon boundary; (2) a reduction in tariffs; (3) an independent treasury system; and (4) the acquisition of California. In negotiations with the British, Polk backed down on his "54°40′ or fight" campaign slogan and settled the Oregon boundary dispute by agreeing to a line running along the 49th parallel, the present border line with Canada. The Treasury system was established in 1846, and the tariff of that same year reduced import duties substantially. Polk was also able to acquire California—as well as the New Mexico Territory —although some historians accuse him of provoking the Mexican War to do so. The conflict was known, even in his own time, as Mr. Polk's War. Polk had sent **Thomas O. Larkin** (*see*) to California with secret orders to stir up a revolt and had ordered Zachary Taylor (1784–1850) to occupy an area near the Rio Grande that was claimed by Mexico and the United States. Polk also offered to buy California and the New Mexico Territory from Mexico, but the offer was spurned. By May 9, 1846, Polk had decided to ask Congress for a declaration of war to recover debts owed to the United States by Mexico. That very night, Polk received word that Mexican troops had attacked Taylor on April 25. War was officially declared on May 13. As a result of the American victory in the conflict, California, the New Mexico Territory, and a disputed portion of Texas were added to the United States. However, Polk, an obstinate leader, was left with few friends and did not seek reelection. He died on June 15, 1849, shortly after leaving office.

PREEMPTION ACT OF 1830. The Preemption Act of 1830 allowed squatters to buy as many as 160 acres of the land they had settled on, at the minimum price of $1.25 an acre. Until then, it was illegal to settle on public land before the federal government had surveyed it and put it up for sale at public auction. However, many settlers ignored the restriction and began farming in any spot they liked. These squatters frequently found themselves dispossessed after their lands had been surveyed because they could not compete with wealthier land speculators who outbid them at public auctions. The Preemption Act was passed by Congress in response to a widespread demand by the squatters in the West. It was later expanded upon in the **Distribution-Preemption Act of 1841** (*see*).

PREEMPTION ACT OF 1841. *See* **Distribution-Preemption Act of 1841.**

R

REMOVAL ACT OF 1830. As a solution to the problems that arose whenever white settlers and Indians came into conflict over Western lands, Congress passed the Removal Act on May 28, 1830. It authorized the President to exchange territory west of the Mississippi for land claimed and occupied by Indians in any state or territory of the United States. The act also authorized the President to transport the Indians at government expense to their new lands. This was often accomplished by brutal means, with Indians being herded into stockades while their homes were ransacked. Northern tribes that were moved west of the Mississippi included

the Winnebagos, Sauks, Potawatomis, and Foxes, all of whom were relocated in present-day Iowa. The Chippewas were transferred to Wisconsin and Minnesota, and the Delawares, Ottawas, Shawnees, Miamis, and Iroquois were removed to the western border of Missouri. Of the Southern Indians, the Five Civilized Tribes —the Seminoles, Cherokees, Choctaws, Creeks, and Chickasaws— were pushed to the area west of Arkansas. The removal of the Cherokees in 1838 was particularly tragic. About 4,000 died on their forced march west, which is known as the Trail of Tears.

ROSE, William (dates unknown). The son of a white trader and a part-Cherokee, part-black woman, Rose was a legendary buffalo hunter, fur trapper, guide, and Indian interpreter in the early part of the 19th century. Details of his early life are unclear. Rose is believed to have first served as a guide for fur companies on several expeditions up the Missouri River after 1807. In the 1820s, he lived with the Crow Indians and later among the Arikaras. In 1823, Rose was a guide and interpreter for the Rocky Mountain Fur Company. Later he went along with **Jedediah Smith** (*see*) on an exploratory and fur-trapping expedition to the Far West. In the 1830s, Rose apparently became a Crow chieftain. Rose's reputation as a scoundrel and an outlaw is based largely on stories about the West written by Washington Irving (1783–1859), but there is no evidence that these tales are true.

S

SACAGAWEA (1787?–1884?). The only female to accompany the

STATE HISTORICAL SOCIETY OF NORTH DAKOTA

Sacagawea

Lewis and Clark expedition (*see*) was a Shoshone Indian whose name, translated, means "Bird Woman." During the journey, Sacagawea served as an interpreter and guide, and her presence with the white explorers assured the Indians along the way that the expedition was peaceful. Sacagawea had been captured at about the age of 12 by a marauding band of Minnetaree Indians. She was traded to a French trapper, Toussaint Charbonneau, whom she later married. In 1805, the couple joined Lewis and Clark at their camp in present-day North Dakota, where Sacagawea gave birth to her first child, Baptiste. The infant traveled with the expedition in a papoose board tied to his mother's back. When Lewis and Clark reached the foothills of the Rocky Mountains, Sacagawea recognized landmarks from her birthplace. They soon met up with a tribe of Shoshones, among whom was her brother, Cameahwait, now the chief. Sacagawea obtained horses from the Indians and journeyed with the explorers to the Pacific. On the way back,

Sacagawea guided Clark to the Yellowstone River. She, her husband, and son left the expedition in the same area in North Dakota where they had joined it. Sacagawea later took Baptiste to St. Louis for Clark to raise. The boy remained with Clark until he was about 19, traveled in Europe, and eventually rejoined his tribe. Many years later, Baptiste was told of an old Shoshone woman who went by the name of Sacagawea and could recite details of the Lewis and Clark expedition. He acknowledged her as his mother. After her death, Sacagawea was buried on the Wind River Indian Reservation in Wyoming.

SANTA FE TRAIL. A famous trade route in the mid-19th century, the Santa Fe Trail extended 780 miles between Independence, Missouri, and Santa Fe, in present-day New Mexico. It was marked out after Mexico achieved independence from Spain in 1821 and announced that American traders would be welcome in Santa Fe. William Becknell (1790?–1832?), hearing of the news, was the first to arrive there with three wagons of merchandise. The route taken by Becknell, who was later known as the father of the Santa Fe Trail, ran across the Kansas plains and along the Arkansas River. It then continued west along the river almost to the Rocky Mountains and swung south to New Mexico. A branch that became popular later cut south from the Arkansas to the Cimarron River and finally rejoined the main trail in northern New Mexico. Before the railroad from Topeka to Santa Fe was completed in 1880, the trail was heavily traveled by wagons carrying manufactured goods west and returning with furs and silver from the Southwest.

SMITH, Jedediah (1799–1831). One of the greatest—but largely unknown—explorers of the West, Smith, a native of New York, began his career at the age of 23 when he joined the Missouri River expedition of General **William H. Ashley** (*see*). Smith then remained in Ashley's employ until 1826, when he and two other traders, David E. Jackson and **William Sublette** (*see*), purchased Ashley's Rocky Mountain Fur Company. For the next four years, Smith traveled throughout the Southwest to trap beaver and barter with Indians for pelts, exploring extensively at the same time (*see pp. 531–538*). About 1824, he guided the first Americans to reach the West Coast through the South Pass of the Rockies. Two years later, he led the first expedition to reach the Spanish settlements in southern California by land from the East. In 1828, he also guided the first pioneers to enter the Oregon country from California. Smith left the Rocky Mountain Fur Company in 1830 and started fur trading in the Santa Fe area of New Mexico. The following year, he was ambushed and killed by Comanche Indians at a water hole near the Cimarron River in southwestern Kansas.

SMITH, Joseph (1805–1844). Founder of the religious sect known as **Mormons** (*see*), Smith grew up in upstate New York among uneducated, superstitious frontier settlers. Beginning in 1820, Smith said he received a number of visits from heavenly messengers, who told him that he was God's prophet. They led him to some mysteriously inscribed golden tablets and helped him to translate them. The resulting *Book of Mormon* (1830), among other things, prophesied Christ's return to Earth and traced the ancestry of the North American Indian to the legendary lost tribes of Israel. Earlier in 1830, Smith had organized the Church of Jesus Christ of Latter-Day Saints and soon attracted hundreds of converts. He had intended to set up a Mormon colony west of the Rocky Mountains, but he was able to lead his followers only as far as Nauvoo, Illinois, in 1839. Although the Mormons prospered here, Smith became increasingly tyrannical. This, combined with his endorsement of polygamy—Smith had 27 wives—made him unpopular among many Mormons as well as outsiders. In 1844, Smith announced his candidacy for President of the United States. While his supporters were away campaigning, a riot broke out that Smith was unable to quell. He and his brother Hyrum were arrested, jailed, and murdered by a mob. Smith's martyrdom reconciled the opposing factions of Mormons, and his successor, **Brigham Young** (*see*), led the group to Utah, where they founded Salt Lake City.

SMITH, Samuel Francis (1808–1895). Smith wrote the words for the patriotic hymn *America* in 1832, while a student at Andover Theological Seminary in Massachusetts. The hymn, sometimes titled *My Country 'Tis of Thee,* was sung to a tune he had found in a German songbook. It was only later that Smith discovered the melody was that of the British national anthem, *God Save the King.* A native of Massachusetts, Smith was ordained as a Baptist minister in 1834. Besides being a pastor, he taught languages at Waterville (now Colby) College in Maine from 1834 to 1842 and was editor of *The Christian Review* from 1842 to 1848. As editorial secretary of the American Baptist Missionary Union from 1854, Smith devoted the rest of his life to writing and editing. He made two trips to Europe and Asia to visit missionary stations in the late 1870s and early 1880s. On his return, he published an account of his travels under the title of *Rambles in Mission-Fields* (1883). Smith coedited the popular Baptist hymnbook, *The Psalmist,* which was published in 1843. He also composed a number of other hymns, including *The Morning Light is Breaking.*

SMITHSONIAN INSTITUTION. The Smithsonian Institution in Washington, D.C., was established by Congress in 1846 as an independent institution devoted to research, publications, and permanent exhibits in the fields of science, art, and the humanities. It was originally conceived by James Smithson (1765–1829), a British scientist. Impressed by the democratic ideals of the United States, Smithson left a large legacy to the American government to set up under his name "an establishment for the increase and diffusion of knowledge among men." The institution has expanded considerably since the mid-19th century, and it now includes a large number of individual museums, galleries, research and education centers, and libraries. Among its most famous departments is the National Air and Space Museum, whose collection includes the Wright brothers' *Kitty Hawk Flyer,* Charles A. Lindbergh's *Spirit of St. Louis,* and the space capsule used by America's first astronaut to orbit the earth, John H. Glenn, Jr. (born 1921). The National Gallery of Art and the Freer Gallery of Art are also divisions of the Smithsonian Institution, which is now maintained by Congressional grants and private contributions.

STANTON, Elizabeth Cady (1815–1902). This militant suffragette crusaded most of her life to secure voting rights for women. Born in Johnstown, New York, she studied law at her father's office, where she found that women were considered inferior to men. She was so determined to end discrimination against her sex that when she married Henry Stanton (1805–1887) in 1840, she had the word *obey* deleted from the wedding ceremony. Mrs. Stanton accompanied her husband to London to an antislavery convention, where she met **Lucretia Mott** (*see*). Both were dismayed to find that women were banned from the conference. Along with Mrs. Mott, she helped organize the first Woman's Rights Convention, in Seneca Falls, New York, in 1848. In the opening address, Mrs. Stanton propounded a "Declaration of Sentiments," modeled after the Declaration of Independence. It stated that all women were created equal to men and should be given the vote. From 1851 until her death, Mrs. Stanton worked with another suffragette, Susan B. Anthony (1820–1906), on behalf of various reforms, including temperance and the abolition of slavery.

STOCKTON, Robert Field (1795–1866). The highlight of Stockton's 39-year career in the navy came as commander of the Pacific squadron during the Mexican War, when he helped win California

NEW-YORK HISTORICAL SOCIETY

Robert F. Stockton

for the United States in a series of land and sea battles. Stockton joined General Stephen W. Kearny (1794–1848) and **John C. Fremont** (*see*) in driving the Mexicans out of California by 1847 and was responsible for installing Fremont as the first civil governor of the new territory. Stockton left the College of New Jersey (now Princeton University) to join the navy when he was 16. He served in the War of 1812 and later in the campaign against the Barbary pirates. In 1821, he represented the **American Colonization Society** (*see*) and secured a territorial concession—later named Liberia—on the west coast of Africa. Stockton promoted the development of naval steamships and spurred construction of the *Princeton,* a warship driven by underwater propellers rather than above-the-surface paddles. Stockton designed the "Peacemaker," a 12-inch gun that exploded on February 28, 1844, killing a number of visitors aboard the *Princeton,* including Secretary of State **Abel Upshur** (*see*). An official inquiry into the accident exonerated Stockton. After retiring from the service, Stockton became a Sen-ator (1851–1853) from New Jersey and during his term introduced the bill that abolished the punishment of flogging in the navy.

SUBLETTE, William (1799?–1845). William Sublette was the best known of five brothers from Kentucky who distinguished themselves as fur traders in the West. After he, **Jedediah Smith** (*see*), and David E. Jackson made a fortune trapping beaver, they bought the Rocky Mountain Fur Company in 1826. They then sponsored expeditions to the Far West in search of fur, and as a result, part of the **Oregon Trail** (*see*) became known as Sublette's cutoff. The three men were the first to take wagons over the Rocky Mountains, thus proving that settlers could make the trip, too. In 1832, Sublette formed a fur trading company with Robert Campbell (1804–1879) that lasted for 10 years. Sublette and Campbell competed with some success against the American Fur Company owned by **John Jacob Astor** (*see*).

SUTTER, John Augustus (1803–1880). On January 24, 1848, gold was discovered on Sutter's estate in California's Sacramento Valley. Sutter tried to keep the discovery secret, but the news was quickly spread by **Sam Brannan** (*see*), an ambitious local businessman. In the furious **gold rush** (*see*) that followed, Sutter's lands were overrun, his cattle were slaughtered, and he was left bankrupt. Born in the German state of Baden, Sutter spent part of his youth in Switzerland and served in the Swiss army. He immigrated to America in 1834, settling briefly in St. Louis. In 1839, he arrived in California, where he was granted permission by the Mexican governor to found a colony at the junction of the Sacramento and American Rivers. As leader of the colony New Helvetia, near present-day Sacramento, General Sutter, as he was known, grew rich from his vast landholdings. When the stampede for gold began, however, Sutter was financially ruined. For many years he tried to get Congress to restore his losses, but without success. In 1864, California awarded him a pension of $250 a month. Sutter later settled in Pennsylvania.

T

TEMPERANCE MOVEMENT. What began in the early 1800s as an appeal for moderate drinking habits became one of the major reform movements in the nation by the mid-century. By then, it had developed into a campaign for laws to end all sales of alcoholic beverages. One of the first reformers to receive national attention was Dr. Benjamin Rush (1745?–1813) of Philadelphia. He gave impetus to the movement by publishing in 1784 a study describing the harmful results of excessive drinking, entitled *An Inquiry into the Effects of Spirituous Liquors on the Human Mind and Body.* America's first temperance society, established in 1808 at Saratoga, New York, was organized by 44 men who pledged to "use no rum, gin, whisky, wine or any distilled spirits." At this time, Protestant churches also began campaigning for temperance, and preachers such as Lyman Beecher (1775–1863) won many parishioners to the cause. Founded in 1826, the American Society for the Promotion of Temperance, also known as the **American Temperance Union** (*see*), held lectures, distributed propaganda, and sent out missionaries to get persons to sign temperance pledges. Converts who vowed to abstain totally from liquor—moderate tippling was permissible at first—placed a capital *T* beside their name and became known as teetotalers. In the 1840s, a group named the **Washingtonians** (*see*) won widespread support by having reformed alcoholics speak against the evils of drink. Temperance crusaders eventually opposed all drinking and began wielding considerable political influence. One of the most widely read books at the time became *Ten Nights in a Barroom* (1854) by **Timothy Shay Arthur** (*see*). Beginning with Maine in 1846, the reformers succeeded in getting prohibition laws passed in 13 states by 1855. Despite this, the reformers made little headway in changing the nation's drinking customs. Many who had taken the pledge returned to drinking, and during the 1850s the temperance movement became temporarily overshadowed by larger national issues, particularly the abolition of slavery.

THOREAU, Henry David (1817–1862). This famous writer, one of the leading figures of the literary and intellectual movement known as **Transcendentalism** (*see*), is best known today for his advocacy of civil disobedience. He believed that a citizen was obligated to break unjust laws, whatever the consequences. Thoreau was born in Concord, Massachusetts, where, except for brief periods, he spent the rest of his life. After graduating from Harvard in 1837—where he achieved no academic distinction but was probably the best-read person in his class—Thoreau became a teacher in the Concord town school. Before the

term was over, he had quit rather than maintain discipline by whipping his pupils. The same year, he and his brother John opened a private school. The curriculum included Latin, Greek, French, and mathematics, and the students were often taken on nature trips. When the school was closed in 1841 on account of John's health, Thoreau went to live in the home of **Ralph Waldo Emerson** (*see*), where he acted as general handyman, continued to write poetry and essays, and even edited Emerson's journal, *The Dial,* on one occasion while Emerson was away. During this time, Thoreau met several members of the Transcendentalist group that surrounded Emerson, including **Bronson Alcott, Margaret Fuller** (*see both*), and George Ripley (1802–1880). Thoreau disagreed with the more mystical aspects of the movement, which did not jibe with his scientific turn of mind. For that reason, he determined to live by himself. In 1845, he built a cottage on Emerson's land on the bank of Walden Pond, just outside Concord. During that summer, he was arrested for refusing to pay poll tax as a protest against the Mexican War. After he spent one night in jail, bail was quickly provided by one of his aunts, much to his disgust. This incident provided the impetus for his essay "Civil Disobedience," first published in 1849. Thoreau spent two years at Walden Pond, observing nature and philosophizing on social problems. His well-known conclusion was that "Our life is frittered away by detail. . . . Simplify, simplify!" He published his theories in his classic *Walden* (1854). Upon his return to Concord in 1847, he spent the next five years tending his herb collection, keeping weather records, and lecturing

and traveling around New England. Although ill with tuberculosis, Thoreau was the first to defend abolitionist John Brown (1800–1859) for his raid on Harper's Ferry in 1859. He died shortly after the outbreak of the Civil War.

TRANSCENDENTALISM. This philosophical movement enlisted the best minds in New England prior to the Civil War and contributed to such reforms as the abolition of slavery. Basically, Transcendentalism was the belief that truth was something each person could sense. The Transcendentalists opposed the widespread notion of their time that knowledge was a product of observation and experience. Such a rational approach, they believed, was intellectually "cold" and mentally limiting. Transcendentalism started in Europe and was made popular in the United States during the 1830s by **Ralph Waldo Emerson** (*see*), whose home at Concord, Massachusetts, became the unofficial headquarters of the movement. Emerson and his followers were convinced that man and nature were unified by the all-embracing divinity of God. In his famous essay "Nature" (1836), Emerson described this unity as the "Over-Soul." The Transcendentalists believed that a person who understood this mystical unity would have revealed to him the essential truths of the universe. Emerson further developed this idea in his 1841 essay, "Self-Reliance." He insisted that "Society everywhere is in conspiracy against the manhood of every one of its members. . . . Whoso would be a man must be a nonconformist." His point was that each person must do what he feels is the right thing to do, regardless of

HOUGHTON LIBRARY, HARVARD UNIVERSITY

This drawing lampoons Emerson's belief in the unity of man and nature.

public opinion. Hence, each Transcendentalist was free to discover his or her own truth—about life, beauty, goodness, even Transcendentalism itself. Transcendentalist thought was published by Emerson and **Margaret Fuller** (*see*) in *The Dial,* a small literary magazine that appeared from about 1840 to 1844. Although the movement was primarily literary, Transcendentalism exercised a considerable influence on the political and social issues of the day. Its emphasis on individual decision and action was especially attractive to the reformers—whether it meant supporting temperance or opposing slavery. In one instance, **Henry David Thoreau** (*see*) went to jail for a day in 1845 for refusing to pay a poll tax in protest of the Mexican War. Today the movement is remembered more for its literary achievements than for its social experiments, which included **Brook Farm** (*see*).

TREATY OF FORT LARAMIE. In 1849, **Tom Fitzpatrick** (*see*), Indian agent of the tribes living near the upper Platte and Arkansas Rivers, asked the federal government for authorization to sign a treaty with the Indians of the area.

Two years later, Congress appropriated $100,000 and made arrangements for a council with the Indians at Fort Laramie (*see pp. 525–526*). Sioux, Arapahos, Cheyennes, and Shoshones gathered that September in one of the largest Indian councils in the West. After 20 days of feasting, hunting and fighting games, and negotiating, a treaty was signed that provided boundaries for each tribe and a $50,000 yearly grant to the Indians. In return, the government gained the right to construct roads and forts in Indian territory. In 1868, a second treaty was signed at Fort Laramie as the result of increasing hostilities between the Indians and railroad construction crews. Under its terms, the Indians promised to stop their attacks on whites. In return, the federal government was to abandon certain forts, restrict the settlement of whites in unceded Indian territory, and establish a Sioux reservation in South Dakota.

TYLER, John (1790–1862). Tyler was the first Vice-President to become Chief Executive on the death of a President. He succeeded William Henry Harrison (1773–1841), who died in April of 1841 after only one month in office. Tyler, who was not popular with his own party, served only one term. Born in Charles City County, Virginia, Tyler was the son of a prominent judge and former governor. He graduated from the College of William and Mary in 1807 and became a lawyer two years later. Entering politics, he served in the state legislature (1811–1816), in the House of Representatives (1816–1821), and as governor of Virginia (1825–1827). Tyler was then elected to the United States Senate as a Democrat in 1827. He resigned in 1836 after breaking

with the Democratic Party over what he considered the unconstitutional policies of President Andrew Jackson (1767–1845). He was again a state legislator (1838–1840) before accepting a place on the Whig Party ticket with General Harrison, the hero of the Battle of Tippecanoe, in 1840. The Whigs carried the nation in the free-swinging "Tippecanoe and Tyler too" campaign that followed. Upon succeeding Harrison, Tyler, the nation's tenth President, found himself frustrated by poor relations with Congress. The Democrats spurned him as a political traitor, while the Whigs regarded Henry Clay (1777–1852), not Tyler, as their party leader. When Tyler, a strong states' rights advocate, vetoed Clay's bill to recharter the Second Bank of the United States, the entire Whig cabinet, except for Secretary of State Daniel Webster (1782–1852), resigned in protest on September 12, 1841. Although Tyler was handicapped by the lack of party support, his administration was marked by the negotiation of the **Webster-Ashburton Treaty** (*see*) in 1842 and the annexation of Texas shortly before he left office in 1845. Tyler returned to Virginia, where he practiced law until 1861. In that year, he supported Virginia's decision to secede from the Union. He was elected to the Confederate Congress but died on January 18, 1862, before he could take office in Richmond.

U

UNITED STATES TEMPERANCE UNION. *See* **American Temperance Union.**

UPSHUR, Abel (1791–1844). Born in Virginia, Upshur was a forceful advocate of states' rights and tried to get the federal government to annex Texas as a slave territory. Upshur served as judge on the Virginia state supreme court (1826–1841) prior to his appointment as Secretary of the Navy by President **John Tyler** (*see*) in 1841. In May, 1843, Upshur was named Secretary of State and began negotiations on the annexation of Texas. He believed that bringing Texas into the Union would strengthen the political security of the South. Before an agreement with Texas settlers could be reached, Upshur was killed accidentally in an explosion aboard the navy warship *Princeton* in the Potomac River (*see* **Robert F. Stockton**).

V

VESEY, Denmark (1767?–1822). A former slave who had purchased his freedom in 1800, Vesey was the leader of an alleged conspiracy to seize Charleston, South Carolina, in 1822. Of about 130 blacks charged in the plot, 37, including Vesey, were executed. A mulatto apparently born in the West Indies, Vesey had been owned by a slave trader named Captain Vesey and for many years sailed with his master on buying trips to the Caribbean. After winning a lottery in 1800, Vesey bought his freedom for $600 and became a carpenter in Charleston. As was the custom in those days, Vesey took his former owner's name as his last name. His first name, originally Telemaque, came to be pronounced and spelled "Denmark." A leader in the African Methodist Church and a powerful speaker, Vesey gradually gathered around him a considerable following of dissatisfied

slaves and apparently kept an arsenal of weapons stockpiled in his home. Vesey mistakenly believed the Missouri Compromise in 1821 meant that slavery was no longer legal anywhere. Together with his followers, he plotted to liberate Charleston's slaves, although it is not clear what he intended to do once control of the city was in his hands. Before an uprising could occur, however, an informer betrayed the group. Vesey defended himself skillfully in court, but in vain. He was hanged on July 2, 1822.

W

WALKER, William (1824–1860). An American adventurer, Walker led a small band of soldiers of fortune in an invasion of Nicaragua in 1855. Joining with native revolutionaries, he seized control of the government and proclaimed himself leader of a new republic. However, Walker's activities angered the Eastern financier Cornelius Vanderbilt (1794–1877). Upset when his business operations in Nicaragua were endangered, Vanderbilt persuaded neighboring Central American nations to overthrow Walker's regime and drive him from the country. Walker, who was born and raised in Tennessee, was an unlikely conqueror. He weighed only about 100 pounds and was homely and shy. He was educated as both a doctor and a lawyer and also became a journalist in New Orleans and San Francisco. Walker first attempted to seize power in northern Mexico in 1853 but was driven out. He went to Nicaragua at the invitation of a revolutionary leader in 1855 and had himself inaugurated as president the following year. Walker's regime was backed by

an American transportation company interested in operating vessels between Atlantic ports and San Francisco, by way of Nicaragua. When a dispute broke out for control of the company, Walker sided with a faction opposed by Vanderbilt. Vanderbilt's agents helped to form the coalition of Latin-American nations that then attacked Nicaragua. An American warship intervened to prevent further fighting, and Walker was sent back to the United States. However, he immediately began preparing a second invasion of Nicaragua. He was on his way there when he was captured in Honduras and executed.

WASHINGTONIANS. The Washingtonians—members of the Washington Temperance Society —were reformed drinkers who traveled throughout the nation holding "personal experience" meetings to win converts to teetotaling. The society, a forerunner of today's Alcoholics Anonymous, was formed in 1840 by a group of Baltimore workmen who frequented the same tavern. Two of them went to hear a temperance speaker one day, and on reporting back to the rest, got into a lengthy argument over the virtues and evils of drinking. Finally, six of the workmen who had drinking problems became convinced that liquor was harmful and decided to form a society to spread the word to others. In their first campaign in New York the following spring, they enlisted 1,800 alcoholics in one week. Similar campaigns were held in every state. The society was particularly effective in reaching persons who did not or could not read the anti-drinking literature published by older temperance societies. Its

One drink led eventually to suicide, according to temperance propaganda.

most famous lecturer was the Reverend Theobald Mathew (1790–1856). Between 1849 and 1851, he reputedly traveled 37,000 miles throughout the United States, winning pledges against drinking from 500,000 Roman Catholics.

WEBSTER–ASHBURTON TREATY. This treaty fixed the northeastern frontier between America and Canada along its present lines and thus settled several boundary disputes between the United States and Britain that had persisted since the end of the Revolution. The treaty, which was concluded in August, 1842, was named for its two negotiators—American Secretary of State Daniel Webster (1782–1852) and Britain's special minister to the United States, Alexander Baring, the First Baron Ashburton (1774–1848). The imprecise wording of the Treaty of Paris of 1783, which ended the American Revolution, had left the exact location of the boundary between Maine and the province of New Brunswick, Canada, unclear. Territorial disputes involving an area of about 12,000 square miles had soon developed between the United States and Britain. According to the terms of the Webster-Ashburton Treaty, an area of more than 7,000 square miles

was awarded to the United States. It included the Aroostook River Valley, where a bloodless border conflict, known as the **Aroostook War** (*see*), had taken place in 1839. Britain was awarded the remaining 5,000 square miles approximately north of the St. John River. In addition, Britain ceded land along the Vermont and New York borders to the United States as well as an area of about 6,500 square miles between Lake Superior and Lake of the Woods. The treaty also granted both nations the right to sail on several waterways, including the St. John River. The Webster-Ashburton Treaty was accompanied by separate diplomatic notes providing for the extradition of criminals and the establishment of a cooperative naval effort to suppress the slave trade off the African coast.

WELD, Theodore Dwight (1803–1895). Weld, the son of a Connecticut minister, was the strongest advocate of temperance in the West and a leading abolitionist leader. As a youth, he was influenced by evangelist **Charles G. Finney** (*see*) and in 1825 joined his "holy band." After preaching in western New York against the horrors of drinking, Weld traveled to England in 1829 to promote the abolition of slavery in the West Indies. He also became an advocate of emancipation in the United States, and with the backing of some New York philanthropists, he helped to found the American Anti-Slavery Society (*see* **abolitionists**) in 1833. Three years later, Weld trained 70 abolitionists who, through a pamphlet campaign, united the antislavery movement in the North. Weld became a lobbyist for abolition in Washington, retiring from public life in 1843 when a strong

abolitionist bloc formed in the Whig Party. In addition to writing many antislavery pamphlets, he was author of *American Slavery As It Is* (1839), which was the basis for *Uncle Tom's Cabin* (1852) by Harriet Beecher Stowe.

WHITTIER, John Greenleaf (1807–1892). Whittier, a protégé of abolitionist **William Lloyd Garrison** (*see*), was one of the leading poets of his day. He came to Garrison's attention when he published his first poem at the age of 19 in the *Free Press* of Newburyport, Massachusetts, which Garrison edited. In 1829, Garrison got Whittier the first of the many editorial positions he was to hold in his career. Four years later, Whittier followed Garrison's lead by publishing an antislavery pamphlet, *Justice and Expediency,* and by joining the abolitionist movement, to which he devoted the next 30 years of his life. Whittier's views were considered so radical that he was twice attacked by mobs. In May, 1838, a group of rowdies burned down the building in Philadelphia from which the *Pennsylvania Freeman*, which he edited, was issued. When Garrison's American Anti-Slavery Society (*see* **abolitionists**) split in 1840, Whittier joined the **Liberty Party** (*see*) and two years later ran unsuccessfully for Congress. Whittier insisted that no compromise should be made on the issue of slavery, and his poem "Ichabod" (1850) was an attack on **Daniel Webster** (*see*), who was attempting to defend the constitutional rights of slaveholders. In 1857, Whittier helped to found the political and literary magazine *Atlantic Monthly.* After the Civil War, Whittier's political activities ceased, but his fame as a poet continued to grow, and many of his best poems were written after this time. Although he published several collections of abolitionist poetry, some of his most famous poems—"Maud Muller" (1867), "The Barefoot Boy" (1855), "Barbara Frietchie" (1864), and "Snow-Bound" (1866) —are about New England life, history, and legends.

WILKES, Charles (1798–1877). Wilkes commanded the first American maritime exploratory expedition (1838–1842) to the Pacific islands, the northwestern coast of the United States, and Antarctica, where Wilkes Land was named in his honor. However, he is perhaps most remembered for his role in the so-called Trent Affair, a diplomatic misunderstanding that almost led to war with Britain. Born in New York City, Wilkes entered the United States Navy in 1818 as a midshipman and studied map making in his free time. Soon after surveying (1832–1833) Narragansett Bay, Wilkes was made director of the navy's Department of Charts and Instruments. In August, 1838, he embarked on his famous expedition with a squadron of six ships and a team of scientists. They charted vast areas of the South Pacific and collected invaluable scientific information. Wilkes' *Narrative of the United States Exploring Expedition* was published in five volumes with an atlas in 1844. He subsequently supervised and edited scientific reports of the expedition, which were published in 20 volumes with 11 atlases between 1844 and 1874. At the outset of the Civil War in 1861, Wilkes, as commander of the *San Jacinto*, stopped the British vessel *Trent* in the Bahama Channel and forcibly removed James M. Mason (1798–1871) and John Slidell (1793–1871), two Confederate commis-

sioners who were bound for Europe. He took them to Boston, where they were imprisoned. Britain strenuously objected to the seizure, but war was averted when Mason and Slidell were released in January, 1862. Wilkes later got into a dispute with the Navy Department and was convicted of insubordination at a court-martial in 1864. He was suspended from duty but later reinstated.

WIMAR, Charles (1828–1862). Wimar, a frontier artist, was born in Germany. At the age of 15, he immigrated to the United States with his mother and settled in St. Louis, Missouri. He was apprenticed to an ornamental artist and in 1852 used an inheritance from a friend to travel to Germany to study painting. It was there that he painted his well-known work, "Attack on an Emigrant Train," which won first prize at the St. Louis Fair in 1869. Wimar returned to America in 1857 and made at least three trips to the headwaters of the Missouri in order to paint Indians. Late in his life, when he was dying from tuberculosis, Wimar was commissioned to paint four historical panels in the St. Louis courthouse. Although he had to be lifted to his scaffold toward the end of the project, he completed it in 1862 and died shortly afterward. The panels were later ruined while being restored.

Y

YOUNG, Brigham (1801–1877). A forceful, practical social innovator of his day, Young succeeded **Joseph Smith** as leader of the **Mormons** (*see both*) and created an unusual cooperative society in the Utah desert. He was raised in the

same part of western New York as Smith and was also a poor farmer. Young often worked as a handyman and at the age of 22 became a Methodist. However, the practicality of Mormonism and its promise of an earthly kingdom for those willing to work for it impressed him. In 1832, he was baptized a Mormon by Smith. Young later led a group of Mormons to Ohio, where he rose in the church ranks and was appointed to the Council of Twelve, the governing body of the church. Young was talented as an organizer and leader of people, but he had no interest in arguing religious theories. After the Mormons moved to Nauvoo, Illinois, in 1838, Young visited England to recruit immigrants for the community. When Smith was assassinated in 1844, Young took over as head of the Mormon Church. He rallied Mormon morale, and realizing that in order to survive the Mormons would have to live apart from those who persecuted them, he decided to establish a separate community in the West. In 1847, Young, with a small band of settlers, arrived in the isolated valley of the Great Salt Lake. He acquired the best lands in the region, planned Salt Lake City, irrigated the desert, and established a self-sufficient economy based on agriculture. Young ruled as a virtual dictator and barred "outsiders" from settling in the community. The United States appointed him the governor of the newly acquired Utah Territory in 1850, but he was removed from office eight years later after he sanctioned polygamy (having more than one wife at the same time) and because of his hostility to non-Mormons. Federal troops took over nominal control of the community, but Young retained actual control until his death.

F. Collier & Son